May you always
Embrace the Beauty
in all things Broken

Breathe

Margaret Cassalina

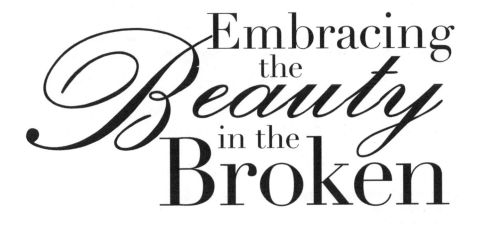

Embracing
the
Beauty
in the
Broken

Margarete Cassalina

EMBRACING THE BEAUTY IN THE BROKEN

iUniverse books may be ordered through booksellers or by contacting:

iUniverse
1663 Liberty Drive
Bloomington, IN 47403
www.iuniverse.com
1-800-Authors (1-800-288-4677)

Because of the dynamic nature of the Internet, any web addresses or links contained in this book may have changed since publication and may no longer be valid. The views expressed in this work are solely those of the author and do not necessarily reflect the views of the publisher, and the publisher hereby disclaims any responsibility for them.

Any people depicted in stock imagery provided by Getty Images are models, and such images are being used for illustrative purposes only.
Certain stock imagery © Getty Images.

ISBN: 978-1-5320-8309-9 (sc)
ISBN: 978-1-5320-8310-5 (e)

Library of Congress Control Number: 2019916416

Print information available on the last page.

iUniverse rev. date: 10/18/2019

Contents

To my husband Marc who, well before I could embrace
it, always saw the beauty in my broken. I love you.

Introduction

Midlife doesn't have to be a crisis. Oh, really? Says who? Says me.

I'm Margarete Cassalina, and I'm a midlife woman who's decided I've had enough crises. It's time I separate myself from crises, both external and internal. Does your inner skeptic think that's not possible?

If you're saying to yourself, "Hmm, that sounds interesting, but I don't know if I could do the same. I mean, after all, how can you avoid a crisis?" then I'm here to tell you that you can. At least you can change the way you deal with your crises. Pull up a chair, grab yourself a cup of coffee, and let's have a little heart-to-heart talk.

> There cannot be a crisis next week. My schedule is already full.
>
> —Henry Kissinger

For all my life, I've had a love of learning, and I'm pretty sure that's why God, in His or Her infinite wisdom and sense of humor, decided to fill the first half of my life with one crisis after another. Through all the trials and many errors, I've come to see that life's challenges, including reaching midlife, don't have to be crises.

Whether you're forty, fifty, or sixty, when that "big 0" birthday comes rolling around, your mind starts grappling with fundamental questions like, "Did I make the right choices in life?"; "Am I going to die with regret?"; "What is my purpose for the rest of my life?"; and "Should I dye my hair or just let it go gray?"

Embracing the Beauty in the Broken is my way of sharing what I've learned and what I'm still working on after four decades of prior living crazy in constant crisis and struggling daily to find calmness and peace of mind. If you've read this far, it's probably safe to say that you've also experienced a crisis or two (or twenty) over the course of your lifetime. Maybe those experiences have taught you precious lessons about life, or perhaps you're still struggling with the curveballs thrown your way. Either way, I'm sure we can agree that these events change you, and when you come out on the other side, you're never the same person as when you first started.

> We have two lives, and the second one begins when we realize we have one.
>
> —Confucius.

Do any of the following descriptions sound like you?

- You're older and wiser, but somewhere rooted in the quiet of your mind you're still wondering if you should be farther along at this stage in your life.
- You find yourself frequently questioning some of the choices you made, especially those that occurred when you were younger.
- You look at all you've accomplished so far but also see all the work that you still want to do. Will you have the time and energy to do it before it is too late?
- You feel hounded by the mental monsters of would've, could've, should've, and what-if. What if I hadn't married that person? If only I could have traveled the world when I was younger. Should I have said yes to that job opportunity instead of the one I chose? What if I had faced my fear, followed my dreams, and lived the life I wanted to? Would my life be different today if I weren't so afraid of failing? What would happen if I put myself first instead of last?

Are these the thoughts and emotions that keep you up at night and drive you crazy? If so, I'm here to help you, and together, with the stories, questions, and discussion prompts in this book, we'll address them one at a time. Remember, as the old saying goes, it's never too late to be who you might have been.

> Someone once told me the definition of Hell: The last day you have on earth, the person you became will meet the person you could have become.
>
> —Anonymous

Sometimes life comes at you fast and a sucker punch lands without any warning. I've been there. I get it. In a split second, you're in the middle of life-changing choices, insurmountable obstacles, and heartbreaking hardships.

Even if a sudden emergency hasn't blindsided you, the daily challenges brought on by everyday life can often be desolating. Maybe you're facing an emotional dilemma with someone who was once close to you. You know you should talk to that person, but you're not feeling ready. Perhaps you've been asked by a friend to take a last-minute trip, or maybe you have an opportunity to start a new job in another part of the country, but you're unsure, needing time to think about it because you're fearful of the unknown, paralyzed by the thought of making the wrong choice.

At each turning point in your life, there's a choice in front of you. Maybe you decide to respond to the family member you're estranged from, or maybe you don't do anything. Maybe you go on the trip or take the job, or maybe you don't. Either way, your life changes course as a result of your choices. However, you are the one who gets to choose how you live your life. Life goes on—until it doesn't.

I know from experience what it's like to take a pass on opportunities. I know what it's like to take action, and I know how it feels when you're face-to-face with time running out. When my daughter, Jena, ran out of time in her battle with cystic fibrosis, my whole world changed. For a long time following that terrible day, it was hard to call up the strength to take action, to move forward, to take a chance at life. Throughout my life, I had been taught to look for and find gratitude in each moment, but when my little girl "moved up" to heaven, there was nothing I could see or find other than my grief and pain. I felt I had no choice.

Through the weeks, months, and years following Jena's passing, I started to understand, again, that life is continually changing and that we have no control over it other than our own thoughts and actions. Change can lead you out of despair or can pull you down with the ship. I made the very conscious decision that change wasn't going to drown me with sorrows. It wasn't easy, but I started swimming against that ocean of pain. Over the years, swimming has made me strong again, and now, many years later, I've come to the place where every day isn't about going against the current. In fact, I think it's safe to say that I now have more days where I feel like I'm floating downstream.

And *that's* why I wrote *Embracing the Beauty in the Broken*.

Despite those feelings of crisis, of fear, of crumbling under life's challenges that have crossed my path so many times, I've learned that I am able to change my life, my attitude, my health, and my mental well-being. Each challenge I faced in life taught me something more about myself and the world around me. Every decision I made, whether I was presented with a multitude of options or no choices at all, changed who I am today.

Here's the thing: somewhere deep in my soul, I know that every journey and every obstacle I faced helped bring me to a place where I can feel calm amid the chaos. Every day I give thanks for a grateful soul, a mind that's confident, and an open heart that's compassionate. If my painful and crazy life journey can reach out and touch your heart in even the smallest way possible and help you deal with and let go of the crises and pain in your life, then I'll feel my words and stories have a purpose beyond what they already hold for me.

Throughout the thirty days and thirty chapters that make up this book, you'll learn how I faced dyslexia, my parents' divorce, leaving home at sixteen, being broke, and having two babies by the time I was twenty-four. You'll discover what it was like for me to learn they were both born with a fatal genetic disease and how I lived despite having debilitating panic attacks and depression. I'll share with you the serious health concerns I've faced along the way and how I've struggled with what my role is in this life I've been given.

Yes, I share some tragically sad stories in *Embracing the Beauty in the Broken*, but I also speak of hope and promise. With each chapter, you'll see the steps I took to take charge of my life and become an award-winning author, a professional speaker, and a national advocate for the Cystic Fibrosis Foundation. I'll share how I've stayed happily married for twenty-eight years to my handsome husband, Marc, and how watching our son marry the love of his life was the best day of mine.

I'll dish out my dirty little secrets along with fun facts like how I went from being too afraid to talk to a computer support technician on the phone to confidently speaking on stage to a crowd of thousands. I'll be honest with you about how I went from living my life for my children to not wanting to live at all. I'll also share the good, the bad, and the ugly when it comes to facing midlife and all its wonders: the hormones, the thoughts about the past, and how to embrace the glorious future that awaits.

I hope that as you get to know me through each new chapter, you'll gain confidence and enthusiasm for opening a new chapter in your life too.

To help you step into your new chapter, I have included three key sections at the end of each chapter: "Here's My Take," "What's Your Take?" and "Take It or Leave It." In the "Here's My Take" section, I summarize the main lessons as I see them. The "What's Your Take?" section then gives you the opportunity to reflect on your life and philosophy and begin thinking about how to apply these lessons in a way that makes sense for you. Finally, in the "Take It or Leave It" section, I encourage you to take action in your own life, and I provide you with exercises and resources, should you want a more in-depth exploration of your own growth and journey.

It's my wish that *Embracing the Beauty in the Broken* inspires positive personal internal development and confidence to live your own best life.

People often ask me, "How did you do it for all those years?" Most of the time I'd tell them that I never wanted to lose the lesson and love that this life has given me and that if I have to face challenges, I'd rather make the choice to do it with a smile and eyes that see the beauty in the world.

I may be the author of this book, but you are the author of your life. As I believe in honesty and transparency, I need to issue a disclaimer and let you know that I am not a professional counselor, doctor, or therapist. I am a mother, wife, and writer who wants to share my heart with yours. Through *Embracing the Beauty in the Broken*, I invite you to join me on the journey of not only my life but also yours. You can digest the thirty chapters one day or one week at a time or binge-read them all in one sitting!

I encourage you to share your thoughts with those close to you, and if you'd like, email me at EmbracingTheBeautyInTheBroken@gmail.com to continue the conversation.

As we journey together, you'll start to see how a challenge doesn't have to be a crisis but rather can be a reminder of the choices we all have to make in this incredible and beautiful adventure called *life*. You might even find that it's the tiny steps, the small acts, the seemingly insignificant decisions, that become the most significant ones, and that through them manifest the most life-changing of all opportunities.

In humor, in tears, and in honesty, I invite you into my life.

Ovulation, Ovaries, and Oh Those Hormones

If I Were a Mood Ring, I'd Be
Flashing Like a Disco Ball

Crisis:
Hormones

Are you there, God? It's me, Margarete.

Yes, I intentionally picked that line from Judy Blume's book to start this chapter. For so many of us in my generation, that book was the go-to source for everything we wanted to know about puberty, sex, and growing up. Except in this version of the story, my name is Margarete, with an *e* at the end, I've just turned fifty, and it's been seventy days since my last period.

Whenever I start having a conversation with God, I feel the need to confess something, and at this point I have to confess that I'm done, with a capital D, with my period. My "friend" has served me well over the last thirty-five years, but now that the end is near, it needs to go away—for good. Just like the fictional Margaret in the *Are You There, God?* story, the relationship I had with my period as a teenager was filled with curious anticipation, the novelty of excitement, and how my changing body defined me among my peers and friends.

Of course, no female coming-of-age story is complete without that "surprise" moment. In my case, Aunt Flo decided to pay her first visit, rather ironically, while I was standing in front of my eighth grade English class presenting my book report on *Little Women*. After the mad dash to the school nurse, I waited in breathless anticipation to be excused early so I could go home, lock myself in the bathroom, and get to know what this new friendship was all about.

Most of my girlfriends had started their periods already, and for months I had felt like I was missing out on something that seemed so adult—they were women, and I was still a girl. But that afternoon everything changed, and I was now getting up close and personal with my very first box of tampons. I read every word and studied the diagram that illustrated the directions. It was rather confusing. I must have spent hours in the bathroom deciding, deciphering, and fumbling in frustration with those cardboard contraptions. It didn't go well, and in the end I opted to break into the massive box of Kotex maxi pads my mother kept underneath the bathroom sink. Clearly, using a tampon was not going to be as comfortable and enjoyable as the TV commercials had led me to believe, and months of trial and error were necessary before I'd get any of it right. In the meantime, I didn't care one bit that I had a mattress-sized maxi pad bunched up in my Hanes cotton undies because, damn it, world, I was now 100 percent officially a woman, complete with acne, braces, a training bra, and now attitude.

The influx of all those hormones impacted every personal relationship I had as a teenager. Hello, short temper! Good to see you, crying fits! Oscillating emotions spewed forth at every turn. It wasn't uncommon for me to say "I love you! No one understands me like you. You're like the best person ever!" and in the next breath scream, "Why would you even say that? You have no idea how important buying those Jordache jeans meant to me. I hate you! I'm never speaking to you ever again!" I never knew when I'd flip out on someone (neither did anyone in my family for that matter) over the slightest annoyance. And everything seemed to be a major annoyance. Yeah, those teenage years were some good times.

Fast-forward several years. It's now November 1990, I'm twenty-two, and there I am in the bathroom holding the drugstore pregnancy test stick that I had just peed on. It showed two tiny lines in the small display window. *Ding, ding, ding! You're the winner, Margarete!* Let me tell you, I *really* missed having my period then. And I continued to miss my period until six weeks after my son was born in July of 1991. But I didn't miss my friend that much, because a little over a year later, I was pregnant once again, and I gave birth to a baby girl in 1993.

After my daughter, Jena, was born, I didn't miss my period again until that fateful day in March when I was forty-eight. I totally freaked out. Could I be pregnant *now*? I know I'm older, but I'm not *that* old. I've read about women having babies in their fifties, and fifty was still two years away for me. Panic started setting in. My period was like clockwork, and I recalled reading somewhere that if you miss a period, you're supposed to see your doctor. Could this be a sign of a health concern? By age forty-eight, I'd had a ton of health concerns, and my mind was racing back and forth between the fear of dying from some horrible disease and being pregnant. Dear God, it's me, Margarete. What the hell do I do now?

I called my new gynecologist. My former ob-gyn, Dr. Rajan, had retired the prior year after being my doctor for thirty years. He stuck with me through those turbulent teenage years, he was my obstetrician for both pregnancies, and he'd helped guide me through a series of scary medical issues I had in my thirties and forties. Dr. Rajan and I had a good thing going, but I wished him well as he rode off into the retirement sunset. But boy oh boy, I was missing him right now. My new doctor, I'll call him Dr. NewGuy, was totally A-OK, but we hadn't been together for long, and our history and understanding of one another, especially my sense of humor, hadn't had time to grow.

Dr. NewGuy's front office wasn't as worried about my impending death or pregnancy as I was. The voice on the other end of the line (kind, but firm) told me to pick up a pregnancy test and come in next week if I still haven't gotten my period.

See? I knew it! They were thinking the same thing I was: I could be pregnant! My next thought was, *Am I happy or sad? Am I excited or scared out of my middle-aged mind?* I didn't have a quick answer for that, but it was an exciting feeling at this stage of my life. What would raising a child later in life be like? I wondered what my now twenty-four-year-old son, Eric, would think. What about my husband, Marc? Oh crap, I've got to call him! He's going to be thrilled by this latest Margarete adventure. But

I'm thinking that as long as it doesn't impact his Wednesday night golf league, he'll be fine. I ran out and bought the same early pregnancy test kit brand as I had bought back in 1990. Once again, I locked myself in the bathroom and carefully read the directions and studied the diagram. Jeez, the print was a lot smaller than I had remembered, and the display window had changed. Instead of one line or two lines, it said "pregnant" or "not pregnant." Well, that was helpful at least.

I followed the instructions and waited the three minutes, wondering what direction our lives would soon take.

Those three minutes seemed like a lifetime as I wondered what life would be like with another child in 2016. Would this child have cystic fibrosis like my two other children? Would I be a more patient parent this time? Would this baby be a little girl or a little boy? What would we name him or her?

Finally, the display appeared. It was undeniable. I let out a heavy sigh and grabbed my phone. "You don't have to quit your golf league, Tiger," I texted Marc at work. "I'm officially old."

I went to see Dr. NewGuy the following week, and he agreed: I'm old. At least that's what it sounded like. He did say something about perimenopause and something else about ovaries, eggs, and hormones. I wasn't listening very attentively until he said that this stage could last up to ten years. Wait, what?! Ten years of living like this? Sympathetic to my blatant ignorance of this stage in a woman's life, Dr. NewGuy gave me the final segment of the birds and the bees talk. Here's the Cliff Notes version: females are born with approximately two million eggs (actually follicles that want to be eggs, but it's close enough), give or take a yolk. By the time my eighth-grade self was fiddling around with tampons in the bathroom, I was already down to about three hundred fifty thousand eggs. Talk about a significant depreciation factor! By the time I was thirty-seven, those egg-wannabe follicles were down to a meager twenty-five thousand. I didn't need a mathematician to tell me what kind of numbers I was looking at for age forty-eight. Picking up a dozen eggs at the grocery store was about to take on a whole new meaning.

Dr. NewGuy told me that over the course of a woman's lifetime, only about three hundred fifty of those wannabe-egg follicles are ever ovulated; fifteen to twenty follicles raced down my fallopian tubes each month to see which little sucker got the honor and distinction of being chosen Queen Egg. Yay! Winner, winner, chicken dinner! Sitting opposite Dr. NewGuy, I leaned across his desk and told him that seeing I only had about a baker's dozen of moldy-oldy egg follicles left, couldn't we just scramble all of them up in one pan and get this whole menopause process over with? Dr. NewGuy didn't seem to get my humor. I'd never missed Dr. Rajan as much as I had at that particular moment. Dr. Rajan would have least given me that courtesy smile of his.

All joking aside, I have to admit it was a very sad and emotional day. When I had texted Marc with my "officially old" comment, I meant it sarcastically, but the realization that there were only so many wannabe-egg follicles left meant there were only so many days in my life left, and that left me shaken and uncertain. In the 1800s, they called this time in a woman's life "the gateway to death" (if you were lucky enough even to live that long), and while I'm glad advancements have improved our life expectancy, the reality was that my physical youth was coming to an end. I figured that by next year, I'd have deep wrinkles, blue hair, and a walking cane. Out of spite, I decided I'd start calling everyone under forty a "young whippersnapper."

The visit to Dr. NewGuy's office had upended my world, but before I left, he had one final bomb to drop: "I'm sorry about having you take that pregnancy test last week. After looking at your chart, I realized you had a tubal ligation at age twenty-five, two endometrial ablations, and a dilation and curettage for abnormal uterine bleeding. There's no way you would have been pregnant."

"Oh yeah, right," I agreed. Somehow I had forgotten almost twenty-five years of my medical history. I guess I'd been distracted by my competing visions of crossing the gateway to death or giving birth to another child. Now I wondered if dementia was starting to set in too.

In the two years that followed the onset of "the change," I had the opportunity to explore some refound youth—like adult acne. That was fun. All those lovely breakouts were kind enough to erupt inside the wrinkles, which was a nice double whammy. Not unlike in my teenage years, my emotional outbursts were spontaneous and a delight for everyone. I wasn't quite as angry as during my youthful days, but I could now sob uncontrollably while scrolling through my Facebook feed. God, grant me a box of tissues if my eyes lingered too long on a post with a Labrador puppy sleeping next to an adorable baby above the caption "Puppy love." I questioned my sanity every single day.

And the "best" part here (I say this with a huge amount of sarcasm) was the enjoyment each month when my ovaries inconsistently decided if I was "egg worthy" or not. That decision or lack thereof hit me with an avalanche of hormones that wreaked havoc on any vacation travel, my sex life, and my once controlled emotional attitude in public. And now when my "frenemy" decided to show up, she placed me on Queen Egg house arrest for days on end. Even those mattress-sized maxi pads weren't enough to deal with what looked like a murder scene escaping from my body. Are you there, God? It's me, Margarete. When is my period going to go away?

❀⁓

Hormones came into my life many years ago, and now they are leaving. My hormones have given me more positives than negatives over the past forty years, and for that I am thankful. They've given me children, a good sex life, and the ability to sleep soundly at night. I've made peace with the fact that my period is coming to an end, and I look forward to the future without it.

But I don't want you to think these few years of going through menopause are nothing but uncontrollable emotional outbursts, unruly chin hairs, and uncontrollable private vacations in the tropics known to others as "hot flashes." While I lament that these bodily changes mean my hair is a bit flatter, my nails more brittle, and my belly puffier, I also have discovered that my "give a damn" is now busted—and that is a beautiful feeling. I don't care as much about all the stuff that used to bother me when I was in my thirties and even my forties. I've made peace with my changing outward appearance, and it feels good. It feels good to let things slide that used to stress me out. Sure, I still get my hair and nails done, and I get a facial now and then because it makes me feel good, not because I'm feeling insecure about who I should be or how I should present myself to the world. I think everyone earns the right to express themselves and feel good in their own skin. Feeling good lowers one's level of stress hormones and strengthens the immune system, and that has to be good for an aging body, right?

Letting go of anxieties and beliefs that used to stress me out has been a big part of my life these days, but don't think for a second that I've stopped taking care of myself or given up on my appearance. No, I'm too vain for that. Seriously. And at fifty I'll be the first to raise my hand and admit it. But the time-management skills I've learned over my lifetime have become a huge help, especially since it now takes me considerably longer to get ready to face the world every day. I need extra time to find a magnifying mirror to apply makeup so I can color inside the lines instead of looking like a clown. I need time to figure out what makeup won't settle in my wrinkles or what eyeliner won't smudge all over my now drooping eyelids. And, yes, I want to focus on the time-consuming process of applying lotions and creams to my dry, cracked, thinned, and creped skin. I've noticed that all my current skin-care purchases begin with two letters: *Re*, as in Resilience, Replenish, Resurface, Replace, Restore, Rebalance, Revive, Reactivate, Rejuvenate, Restore ... This makes buying products for my mature skin easy-breezy. I look for the *Re* and throw it in my bag. It's like the mix-and-match Garanimals clothing I used to wear as a kid, but for my face and skin, with every tube and jar designed to recover the youthful vitality rapidly disappearing from my face and body.

I recently saw a meme on Facebook that said, "Middle age is that time in your life when you finally get your head together, but your body starts falling apart," and while I think that's funny and true, I'm also aware that old age, or even middle age, isn't gifted to all. My daughter, Jena, moved up to heaven before getting her first period, and in all the photographs I have of her, there will never be a wrinkle; her face will always be pure and smooth with the bloom of youth. I painfully acknowledge that despite my current attempts to fade them, the age spots on my hands are a time-stamped mark showing I've been on earth for a long time. And for that I am blessed and give thanks every day.

Here's My Take

In life, there's always a beginning and an end. We have the joyous start of something new and the sad realization of when it's time to say goodbye. We are quick to embrace the happy times, and perhaps we hang on too long to the inevitable goodbyes because we don't want to feel sadness. But if we could look at our goodbyes or endings and all the grief and know that on the other side something new is waiting for us, we might start to understand that every ending is the beginning of something else. My youthful ovaries were a source of strength and power over the years, but now it's time for me to take the reins and provide the vitality and support I need. Now is the time for me to figure out how to use my knowledge, experience, and wisdom to live the best possible life that's ahead of me.

What's Your Take?

Is there anything you're hanging on to that perhaps you should be letting go of? Is it time to part ways? Is the hanging on preventing you from another new adventure? What if we all were like Elsa from *Frozen* and decided to *let it go*? On the flip side, what new experiences are in front of you, or what are some things that you'd like to try? Where can you add more hellos to your life?

Take It or Leave It

Start a notebook or start a Word doc. Take an inventory of things that are leaving or staying in your life at the present time. Next to each thing mentioned, ask yourself how you feel about it. The inventory list is yours, so it should be as long or short as you'd like. This first exercise is just to start thinking about any shifts that are occurring in your life. Acknowledgment is your first step.

I invite you to send me an email at EmbracingTheBeautyInTheBroken@Gmail.com and let me know your story or just share your thoughts about making the shift. I'd love to hear it. We all have a story worth sharing. We truly do.

Is it too early to share just yet? Then contemplate some thoughts on your own, and we'll meet up in the next chapter to talk about being overweight and out of breath.

Overweight and Out of Breath

I Try to Avoid Things that Make Me Fat, Like Scales, Mirrors, and Photographs

Crisis:
Insecurities about My Weight and Appearance

I'm ten years old and in fifth grade, and I'm picked second to last to play dodgeball in gym class. I am one of the three kids, the same three kids who are always picked last for any team sport. None of us can run the warm-up quarter-mile lap around the outside track. We've never run it; we couldn't, so we walked as fast as we could, huffing and puffing, as we watched the rest of the class easily cross the finish line. When we finally finished the lap to meet up with our class, we were always the ones breathing the hardest.

At that age, I had something in common with my mother: we both wore women's size 5 for clothes. But that's where the similarities ended. I was already an inch taller and ten pounds heavier. How do I know this? It's the same year I started keeping a journal that I bought at my local Barnes and Noble bookstore. It had a picture of a beach sunset that I thought was very pretty, and the fact that it had a lock with a removable key made it worth the $4.99. That journal and the many more that followed over the years became my secret refuge for all the thoughts and feelings that ran rampant in my head. I felt no one I knew would be able to understand what I was going through as I struggled with the voices in my head telling me I would never be thin enough, pretty enough, smart enough, or good enough for anyone, especially myself.

As I went from age ten to eleven, I grew into a women's size 7. My dad's affectionate nickname for me was Pork Chop because I liked to eat. Vegetables weren't my favorite, but if you coated them in breadcrumbs, fried them, and served them with a side of ketchup, I'd manage to choke them down. My mother called me Big Oaf. *Husky* was how the doctor classified me. *Big-boned* was my grandmother's preferred term. However, in reality, I was none of those names. I was a kid who grew tall and ate my feelings. I was admired for always cleaning my plate, something I could beat my older and much smaller sister at every time. Confused by the mixed messages, I developed a distorted mental image of myself by comparing myself to my sister, my mother, and my grandmother, all of whom were 5'0" or shorter and weighed under 110 pounds.

By the time I was fourteen years old, I was 5'7" and wore a size 14, and I seriously started thinking that I had been adopted. At that point, I just assumed each clothing size was equivalent to an age. You know, like 3T was for a three-year-old toddler. I figured 15 would be my next size as I continued to eat my feelings and grow and grow.

Be mindful of your words. Words thrown without thought will leave your mind as quickly as you say them, but they have the power to inflict a lifetime of pain.

For many women, weight is so much more than a number on a scale; it's how you compare yourself to the outside world. It's how you compare yourself to other women. Face it, you do. Thinking you're too small or too big is often defined by your comparing yourself to others. You're smaller than this woman; you're larger than that woman. Most of us compared ourselves, and perhaps still do, to friends, family, and those celebrity people with glam squads, personal chefs, and one-on-one personal trainers—and doing such a thing is so distorted and intrinsically harmful. All those comments I heard as a child about being too big, I believed they were true. They weren't. I believed what other people told me, what they said about me, and what they called me because they were adults and I trusted them. That belief had a significant impact on how I saw myself in relation to the world. Those influences fed my insecurities, and in hindsight and through therapy, I see that they were not the best foundational building blocks with which to go through life.

The fact was that when I was ten years old, the health chart at the doctor's office said I had the height and weight of a fourteen-year-old. At fourteen, my height and weight were considered to be adult (i.e., over twenty). But in my homelife, I was compared to the females in my thin, short-statured family. The reality that I was a fairly appropriate size for my height would never penetrate the mental distortion I had of myself or the terms of endearment bestowed upon me as a child.

Even if my weight-to-height ratio wasn't unhealthy, my eating habits were. As a child and as an adult, eating has always been something I love to do. I never understood when people would say they couldn't eat another bite because they were full. I never realized what being full had to do with eating. My memory is that I received positive comments, accolades even, for cleaning my plate. I was the good girl you could feed anything to, and I would eat it. I've always liked to make people laugh, so as a kid I'd leave notes on my grandmother's fridge that read: *Contents: Empty. Sorry, I Ate It All!* My grandmother loved getting those and joyfully referred to them for decades. You can see why I have positive thoughts about making people happy by eating really well.

My favorite foods were high in sugar: cereals, loaves of white bread, pastries, and anything milk chocolate. I ate all my Halloween candy within twenty-four hours because I could not stop. I'd even down the Necco wafers and candy corn no one else wanted. When my grandfather would visit, he'd bring one of those huge one-pound, Hershey's chocolate bars. I'd easily finish it off before I went to sleep that night, though I tried so hard to save it. My childhood dream wasn't to marry Prince Charming but to consume an entire tray of warm, chewy, gooey chocolate chip brownies right out of the oven. The smell has always been one of my favorites. I never did eat that entire tray of brownies, but I have come close a few times. Willpower never worked for me as a kid. It still doesn't.

Serving size was up for grabs. I remember coming home from high school, plopping down in front of the TV to watch *General Hospital*, and eating an entire box of Apple Jacks breakfast cereal with half a cup of skim milk. I thought that since it had apple in the name, it was a healthier choice over Lucky Charms with marshmallows. Skim milk was a conscious choice because I was watching my fat intake after being told how fat was terrible to eat.

But it wasn't just my bad eating habits that were the reason why I was always out of breath, or why I got light-headed, or why I'd regularly pass out in the shower. It wouldn't be until many years later that I'd learn I was born with a hole in my heart, a patent foramen ovale (PFO), and that it was a ticking time bomb just waiting to cause a major health crisis when I hit the big 3-0.

> A figure with curves always offers a lot of interesting angles.
>
> —Wesley Ruggles

As a teenager and young adult, I didn't make excuses for being out of shape. I thought I was just fat. I spent many hours, and all kinds of money, reading every self-help book I could get my hands on to fix my weight problems. I thought the number on the scale was my only issue. I would do anything and everything to adjust that number. As it turned out, reducing that number on the scale was the least of my worries.

By eighth grade, I was throwing up food so I wouldn't gain the weight. A girlfriend and I ate a whole jar of Jif peanut butter with Nestlé's semisweet chocolate chips and made ourselves throw it up, at first with our fingers and then with a toothbrush. That was just the beginning of my eating disorder. I graduated middle school and started high school taking Ex-Lax and Dexatrim, a laxative and an over-the-counter diet pill, respectively, to lose weight. I knew it was wrong, but I didn't care. It seemed the best alternative to being called names like Thunder Thighs and hearing mimicked noises of the ground shaking as I'd walk by. Yes, that was what kids in high school used to do as I walked by. I tried to fix the size of my jeans and the number on the scale, but I didn't know to fix the distorted mental image I had of myself. I cared more about what other people thought of me. I cared more about fitting in and not being called names. I cared more about what the outside world labeled me as than what I thought of myself. Quite frankly I didn't think much of myself. No one said I was worth more than the number on the scale. No one told me I had a value that couldn't be seen.

This, my friends, was my first crisis. I believed I was fat, alone, and unworthy. And the world seemed to validate that.

A negative self-image reflects the insecurity that lurks just beneath the surface. As an adult, I've known gorgeous women who hid their dangerous distorted mental images of themselves underneath their own perceived "perfect" size 2. At the time, I would negatively shrug them off as being perfect and ignorantly judge that being thin and beautiful was easy for them. I'd tell myself that they didn't know how hard it was to diet. I'd convince myself they were born that way, and I'd be full of envy. It was easy for me to judge them and denounce their path because I was struggling so hard with my own body image. I did not realize I wasn't the only one with a hidden distorted mental image. Mental self-abuse comes in all sizes. At the time, it was inconceivable to me that the women I may have judged so harshly were battling their own demons. To this day, I hold remorse that I judged others as harshly as I judged myself.

For me, eating alone in front of a TV with a box of cereal, a loaf of Wonder Bread, and a jar of sugar-free strawberry jam was not the real problem. It was the only solution I had come up with so I could ignore my emotions. Dear Lord, the thought of what I did to myself back in those days makes my stomach turn and my heart weep.

The first line of defense is to address the underlying cause, and the second is to face reality. Was I overweight? Yes, to a certain degree. Was I unhealthy? Absolutely. Was either of those issues addressed while they were happening? No. Am I repeating those same mistakes now? No. I regret that my parents allowed the initial problem to blossom, but once I became an adult, it was up to me to change for the better. I had to take responsibility to face reality and go in the direction that would help me to become healthy. Each day I wanted to be mentally and emotionally better than I was the day before. And at some point I stopped blaming my parents, believing they'd done the best they could've with what they had.

At some point, you want more for yourself than what you have. At some point, it's your responsibility to figure out how to make your life better. When I was a young adult, the place to figure that out was the self-help section of a bookstore or library. Today we have a wealth of knowledge at our fingertips; it's called Google, and it can be used to create powerful change in your world.

> Your genetics loads the gun, and your lifestyle pulls the trigger.
>
> —Mehmet Oz

Once I got married and had children, I stopped the purging, the laxatives, and the diet pills, and instead became addicted to every fad diet that magazines touted as the next greatest weight loss solution. I went from eating tons of cheese, eggs, and meat on Atkins to gallons of diet cabbage soup. There was something I enjoyed about the colorful balance of the South Beach Diet, but I did not like calculating all the points for every little bite on Weight Watchers. Through it all, I was still determined to fix the "problem" of the number on the scale. I didn't care about muscle mass, body fat, or other health issues. I hadn't learned the value of my blood sugar number or my cholesterol level, or what triglycerides were (unbeknown to me at the time, mine were exceedingly high at 350). The number on that almighty scale was the only number that mattered. I didn't know the value of sound mental health and emotional well-being. I wanted to lose weight fast and didn't put too much weight (pun intended) on anything else. I was young and naïve, but I was about to get schooled big-time.

By the time I hit the big 3-0, I had been married for eight years and had two children diagnosed with cystic fibrosis. That was also the year I had a ministroke, which landed me in the hospital. While I was in the hospital, I was diagnosed with prediabetes and hypertension, and my BMI was 25, which put me in the overweight category. On top of that, the hole in my heart, a PFO, a patent foramen ovale, was also discovered.

Earlier that day my husband, Marc, had noticed that my speech was slightly slurred. I told him I wanted to go to sleep, but the words came out all garbled. As I attempted to go upstairs to bed, I tripped not once, but several times before I made it to the top. Thank God Marc quickly gave me two aspirins and called the doctor, who told him to take me to the ER immediately. In the ER, I was told I had a transient ischemic attack (TIA), sort of a ministroke. Through a series of tests with neurologists and cardiologists, it was determined that the TIA had been caused by a blood clot reaching my brain due to the hole in my heart. The cardiologist put me on a blood thinner and a beta-blocker. He also told me I had a high probability of having a full stroke within five years if I didn't take my physical health more seriously. He told me I'd been lucky, very lucky, this time.

If there's one thing I am, it's an "all in" type of gal. When I was released from the hospital, I knew I had to get serious about my eating and lifestyle, so I decided I was going to start running. Because I had never been able to run, in my mind runners were the perfect role model of physical health. I started putting the feet on the pavement, and on a good day, if I pushed myself, I managed a slow jog that was more like a fast walk. But it was hard, and my motivation flagged. The weeks turned into months and then into years, and while I was getting healthier, I was still not exercising as I should have been. One morning, I found myself struggling with my daughter, Jena, to get her to do her morning breathing exercises. Having a routine that strengthens the lungs is critical for kids with CF, but I suddenly saw how my excuses and delays in caring for my own health were setting a bad example. If I expected Jena to exercise, I needed to exercise. I may have been born with a hole in my heart, but she had been born with two severely compromised lungs. We both needed to do all that we could to offset our genetics.

So the two of us started walking. That winter, I announced I would run the quarter-mile loop around the nature trail near our house in Florida, the same distance as the track from my childhood. This time I set small goals to achieve my renewed goal of becoming a runner. My first small goal was to run the hundred feet from the entrance of the trail to the first garbage can. I ran full speed, but by the time I reached the can, I was so out of breath that I panted as I walked the rest of the trail. The next day I slowed my pace a little and made it to the garbage can and a few steps beyond. The next goal was to run to the park bench that was about one hundred feet beyond that. All winter long, I did this with Jena by my side encouraging me, telling me that I could do it. And this time I believed that I could. This time, I was going to do it.

As the winter wore on, my strength and stamina increased, but Jena's did not. On days when she couldn't run or walk, she rode her bicycle instead. She was my biggest cheerleader and my most inspiring personal trainer. By the end of that winter, I had done it. We had done it. At thirty-five, I ran a quarter mile for the first time in my life. The ten-year-old inner child had finally tackled lifelong internal doubt about what was possible. I could run. Running that distance was my proof that I could overcome my self-imposed limitations and that through consistent daily action, I could reach realistic goals. I was healing the insecure little girl inside me, and it felt good.

The following year, my goal was to run a full mile, and Jena was there for me. By this time in her life, her lung functioning had declined to 19 percent, so her bicycle was replaced with a motorized scooter. Still, being out in the fresh air and shouting words of encouragement was good for her, and together we started to overcome what we thought we couldn't do. We worked on overcoming obstacles every single day until the day came when even our most committed efforts were not enough to overcome Jena's disease, for which there was no cure.

When Jena moved up to heaven in 2006, I stopped running. I gave up on everything. I gave up on taking care of myself. There was just no point. Her life had ended, and I chose to stop caring about my life, too. I lived that way, just going through the motions, until a year later when I was in Florida and accidentally drove past the nature trail. The emotions were so overwhelming that I stopped the car, got out, and just started to run. I ran hard, and I ran fast. I ran past the garbage can, past the bench, and past the exit and continued running, crying every single step of the way. In my mind, Jena's voice kept saying, "Mommy, you can do it! Keep going, Mommy!" By the time I was done, I had run over three miles. Sweating, crying, and overcome with tears, I collapsed in the grass. I was exhausted, broken, and ashamed. We had worked so hard together to live life to the fullest, to fight against what we'd been dealt, and in my grief, I had insulted her fierce fight to live by giving up on myself. I had done a disservice to her spirit by letting myself fall apart—again. At that moment I knew I needed to change myself for the better, for the last time. I knew that I could. I'd do it not only for her memory but also for my health.

Even though it's been thirteen years since that fateful day, I'm pleased to report that I still run on a regular basis, both outside and at the gym. In the last few years, Marc and I have also taken up extreme hiking. And by extreme, I mean we've hiked the Grand Canyon in *one* day, rim to rim, twenty-seven miles with twelve thousand feet of elevation change, in hundred-degree weather. As of today, we've done that hike twice. We also did an extreme hike in Mammoth Lakes, California, for a total of twenty-three miles in one day. This year we've signed up to do two this summer. Why on earth would we do this? I do it for my health, but also for raising funds and awareness for the Cystic Fibrosis Foundation and the thirty thousand children and adults living with cystic fibrosis. These extreme hikes are anything but easy, and they're a real test of my stamina and endurance. But when the going gets rough on the trail, I tune into the voice Jena, who even in spirit is still my favorite personal trainer: "Mommy, you can do it!" Even after all these years, she's still in my heart and in my head, and together there's nothing we can't do.

Here's My Take

Since that three-mile run through that nature trail in 2007, my weight is no longer an issue. I had to address my distorted self-image and stop comparing myself to people who were nothing like me. I had to learn to ignore the number on the scale. I have health issues I was born with, and early on I made bad lifestyle choices that led me to be overweight, unhealthy, and prediabetic. But I chose not to use my medical problems as an excuse for poor health. Diets set me up for failure, so I'd rather change my lifestyle to the 80/20 rule: 80 percent of the time I eat and exercise well so that 20 percent of the time, like at Sunday family dinners and on Friday date nights, I can eat foods I don't normally consume. I feel so much better mentally and physically. Life is about balance, and perfection is a goal we can never and should never attain. I still eat what I want, when I want, but the choices are a bit different. Like right now as I am writing this chapter, I finished two large glasses of water and half a bag of Beanitos, tortilla chips made out of pinto beans. I still love to munch, but I try to make better choices. Fewer carbs, higher fiber, a little protein, and no gluten makes my body feel its best. My goal now is to enjoy life, a balanced life.

What's Your Take?

Are you an apple comparing yourself to an orange? Are you comparing your worst faults to someone else's best attributes? It's not always easy to look in the mirror and say, "Damn, I'm doing just great today!" But when you get there—and you will—you'll proudly acknowledge your success and know just how hard you worked on yourself to get there. Being proud of your accomplishments is vital to your own mental health. You can accomplish what you set your mind to. What one thing have you been putting off or think is out of your reach? What is the first memory you have of when you were young and felt the world spinning out of control? Was there a time when you thought you were alone and unable to share your pain with someone for fear of being judged? What would you say to the young you now if given a chance to go back in time and give advice? Would you take, or are you taking, that advice right now as an adult?

Take It or Leave It

Decide for yourself what enough is. Know it. Own it. Be real about it. Pick one thing that's been hanging over your head that you'd like to change, or pick a goal you really want to achieve but have up until this point felt was out of reach. Pick a date when you'll stop making excuses and take your first small step. Take that step and mark it on your calendar or in your journal. And then plan the next step. You can do it. If this Pork Chop can do it, you most certainly can.

Join me in the next chapter and find out why it's better to be alone than to be with someone who makes you feel empty and deserted. Define your values, know your worth, and get ready to turn the page.

Over and Out

Crisis: Abandonment

Being divorced is like being hit by a Mack truck. If you live through it, you start looking very carefully to the right and to the left.

—Jean Kerr

I am a child of parents who got divorced when I was in the eighth grade. I think many kids would want their parents to stay together, but I always prayed mine would go their separate ways. I was tired of feeling like I should take sides. I was tired of going to bed covering my ears with a pillow just so I could hear my own thoughts. I was tired of wondering if I had done something wrong.

At thirteen, my world had simple rules, but my emotions were complex, and I didn't quite understand them. Life to me at that age was black and white, and someone had to be right, which meant that someone had to be wrong. But that thought left me very conflicted. And depending on the day, that meant to my young mind that if one person was right, then the other one was wrong. I was confused in thinking I might have had something to do with their divorce. The only way I could make sense out of what was happening was to look at things the only way I knew how, in black and white, winners and losers, right and wrong, together or broken. At that time, the only thought I had was that I was completely broken. That year I began to have insecurities about the world around me. I no longer had a sense of security, I had feelings of abandonment, and I felt as though I was disposable like last week's rotting garbage, easily tossed and discarded.

Although everyone in our family gradually adjusted to a new normal, the divorce changed everyone, my father, mother, brother, and sister, for better or for worse. For me, it changed where I lived. The summer I turned thirteen was the year I went to live with my father's parents. It was exactly what I needed to help me deal with the uprooting of my family, and I got to reinvent myself at a new school. I also got wholesome nightly meals that included a baked potato at every dinner, and no fighting and no slamming doors. The year I lived with my grandparents, my grades improved, my health improved, and the nickname they called me was Love Bug. Just writing that term of endearment still makes me smile because it was said to me with such love and kindness toward my soul— and it had nothing to do with food or any of my physical attributes.

My grandparents gave me a sense of being unconditionally loved, and as enjoyable as the time was with them, I still wanted to come home when the school year was done. "Home" now consisted of my mother, my sixteen-year-old sister, and my two-year-old baby brother. I saw my father on weekends where he would take us to play video games at the local arcade and then have dinner at McDonald's. I never really liked the arcade or video games, but he and my sister had fun challenging each other to Pac Man, Space Invaders, Formula One car racing or whatever the latest game was in the early eighties. I was holding out for the reward of dinner at McDonald's. I'd sing the McDonald's theme song in my head while they'd race each other around the simulated track of Monte Carlo. "Two all-beef patties, special sauce, lettuce, cheese, pickles, onion on a sesame seed bun ... Yum." I knew a Big Mac and a large order of salted fries were well worth my patience. You bet I ate the whole thing and anything that was left over from my sister.

Life at home became emotionally tense once my mother started dating, so when I had the opportunity to move to Germany the following year, I jumped at the chance. My mother's aunt Thea was willing to take me in for a cultural experience. Living in Germany sounded like the perfect escape from home, so I packed my bags as fast as you can say, Gesundheit! The few friends I had at school wished me well and promised to send letters while I was away—it was the 1980s after all. Email? No such thing existed. So that meant handwritten notes on stationery and airpost stamped envelopes. As much as I love the convenience of email, text, and FaceTime, a part of me misses using penmanship and sitting down to write a letter. It's a lost art, don't you think?

Living with my great-aunt Thea in Worms, Germany, gave me yet another chance to reinvent myself. My aunt wasn't as loving or affectionate as my grandparents, but she provided a very kind, yet structured and meticulous, environment. The best part of living with her was that she was a fantastic baker. I never went without delicious cakes or pastries after dinner, and every breakfast consisted of soft-boiled eggs, toast with jam, and a variety of meats and cheeses. As in years past, I was given positive compliments for eating all my food. My clean plate award streak remained unbroken, and I was now a record holder in two countries.

In Germany, I went to school Monday through Saturday, with the Saturday school day lasting until noon. Saturday afternoon was spent making the house spotless, including cleaning the silver and pressing the cloth napkins and the linens. Great-Aunt Thea never used paper napkins or place mats. We did all this work on Saturday because Sundays were days for rest. You couldn't run the vacuum, sweep the steps, or even go shopping because all the stores were closed. Sunday was a time when everyone was to be home with their families, resting and relaxing with one another and eating.

I'd moved to Germany despite knowing only a few phrases I had picked up from listening to my mother talk with my grandmother, so it was initially hard to communicate with people and the kids at school. Going to the Gymnasium (pronounced "Gim-nah-zeeum"), the German name for a high school, provided an opportunity to use my mime skills and hand gestures to interact with the locals and the kids in my class—sometimes with unexpected results. One time I was tapping my forefinger to my temple as if to say *I'm thinking,* but my new German friend interpreted it as calling her stupid or crazy. After giving me an "I don't think you know what you're doing!" look, she educated me on what my hand gestures meant in this country. There was plenty I needed to learn and change if I was ever going to have a chance at fitting in. I quickly learned to hold my thumbs rather than cross my fingers when wishing for a positive outcome for something. Nothing bonds two teenagers more than speaking in silly hand gestures for an afternoon, especially when we discovered that flipping the bird and giving the finger crossed our cultural lines. Fortunately it wasn't long before I could understand most of what everyone was saying, and my vocabulary improved.

Since my aunt worked long hours as a taxi driver during the day, I quickly became self-sufficient and rode my bicycle around Worms or traveled to the adjacent towns of Mannheim, just fifteen miles south, and Mainz, about thirty-five miles north, on the train. My favorite trek was to the local bakery, or die Bäckerei, where I'd eat as much Kuchen (cake) as possible for two deutsche marks.

Despite enjoying my new friends and freedom, the letters I received from friends back in the States made me homesick. After seven months and much deliberation, I moved back home. The home I returned to was not the same one I had left, but then again, I was not the same girl who had left. A chubby new me returned home to live with my small-framed, hundred-pound mother. I was now fifteen, I had gained twenty-five pounds, and most of my childhood friends greeted me with, "Wow, you got fat!" During the time I was gone, my little brother had moved five hours away to live with my dad, and my sister had moved out of the house as well. Even though I had become more independent in Germany, I still longed for a family that no longer existed. Every time I relocated, I searched for a sense of belonging, but instead I just felt a sense of abandonment. The thought of being like disposable trash surfaced once again in my head. I continued to struggle with insecurities, and they, along with the number on my scale, continued to grow.

> Remember that children, marriages, and flower gardens
> reflect the kind of care they get.
> —H. Jackson Brown Jr.

Because of the German school curriculum, I discovered I was on track to graduate from high school a year early. I was excited about this. As a 5'7", 160-pound 16-year-old taking advanced classes, I fantasized that graduating would remove all my insecurities and that my problems would magically disappear. The fairy tales I created in my mind about the future made sense to my adolescent brain. So did falling head over heels in love. Well, at least I thought it was love. Whatever it was, it sure took up a lot of my time and energy, and a huge part of my diary. Young love will alter any young girl's direction, and I was no different. My grades rapidly deteriorated. My mother had attended and graduated from Vassar College, a prestigious liberal arts school in New York, and she had expected I would do the same. But with my attention on love rather than my academic future, a college like Vassar was soon out of the question. In the fall of 1985, though leaving high school a year earlier than my classmates, I enrolled as a freshman at the local community college.

I felt like I was such a disappointment, and I didn't know how to reinvent myself to become the kind of person I thought I was supposed to be. One day in June of 1985, I vividly remember seeing the open front door. At age sixteen, with nothing but my clothes and my old VW Jetta nicknamed the Orange Crush, I left my mother's house for the very last time. I never did go back into her house again. My insecurities were validated as I left home with my entire life stuffed in a black Hefty garbage bag as she shut the front door behind me. Irony at its best.

Lonely is not alone; it's the feeling that no one cares.

(For further, detailed information about my childhood, please refer to my memoir, *Beyond Breathing*, iUniverse, 2008.)

Here's My Take

We are not our past, but surviving our own history makes us who we are. We are the sum of our past, and I don't think that's a bad thing. Our past has led us directly to where we are today.

They say that kids adapt to divorce, and I would agree. I adjusted to what life gave me, but my parents' divorce changed me. Any sense of security or belonging slowly dissipated. The young love didn't last long after high school, and once again I went out in the world to reinvent myself in different cities, at different colleges, with different jobs, and in different relationships. Nothing stuck for long except my abandonment issues, and those were a very heavy weight deep down in my soul. I decided that I would depend on no one but myself and hide my feelings of loneliness. I just wanted to be alone, so I began to build walls around myself to keep me from getting hurt.

During this self-imposed alone time, I had a lot of conversations with myself. I read self-help books and tried to find some direction that would heal me. If there was anything I learned, it was that victims rarely recover and that wallowing in a self-pitying mind would only set me up for future mistakes and misfortunes. Even if I didn't want to, I had to take responsibility for my life. Sure, I felt a need to blame others at times, but doing that was only going to keep me in a rut and make me miserable. I was committed to moving forward with my life. Unlike Humpty Dumpty, I was going to pick up those pieces and put myself back together again.

One of the things I remember most about this period was that I learned it was better to be alone with my thoughts than to be lonely in the company of people who didn't value my heart, my mind, or me. I learned that distractions were just that—distracting—and that they would keep me from moving forward in my life. I learned that solitude was a place to hear your thoughts and to pray, even though I had never learned any official prayers. I quietly sat and talked to the heavens above, asking for help and hoping to be able to share the love I had inside me with someone and receive that kind of love in return. I learned to love myself enough to want better for myself. The time I spent rebuilding helped me realize I was stronger than I'd thought I was. I learned to be comfortable and accept my thoughts and feelings. I learned that beauty truly comes from within and that I was beautiful, too, in my own broken and cracked sort of way. But all that took years, if not decades, to understand.

What's Your Take?

We all have times in our lives when we feel abandoned or when we're facing the world all alone. Were you working hard at wanting to belong, to fit in, or to be part of the norm, but dealing with curveballs you were incapable of hitting? Have you ever felt like Humpty Dumpty after he took that big fall, your life in pieces, strewn about on the ground? What did you do to piece yourself back together?

Take It or Leave It

Grab that handy-dandy notebook and jot down a few things you love about yourself. I know it sounds silly, but do it. First, write down the things you've accomplished, and then write down the things you enjoy doing all by yourself. Perhaps you like reading, writing, painting, or maybe even dancing alone in the kitchen. Finally, write down the dreams and goals you have for yourself, whether for tomorrow, the next year, or the next decade. When you put it all down on paper, the words about who you are, where you've been, and where you'd like to go will show you the path of action you need to take to achieve what it is that you want to have in your life.

Once you start to follow your path to joy and self-worth, you'll be surprised by the doors that open and the opportunities that present themselves.

Here's something else to try if you're not ready to write yet. Start each day by smiling at the mirror for a minute while practicing the 3:1 rule: tell yourself one thing you like about yourself, one thing you're going to accomplish today, and one dream you are working toward. Remember to have gratitude for what you already have in your life, with the number one thing being you!

When you begin to own the strength and beauty that's within, you'll no longer want to be surrounded by people, behaviors, and actions that bring you down and make you feel unimportant. I'll show you how this manifested itself in my life in the next chapter. I realized that love doesn't always present itself with wine and roses. Sometimes it shows up at the mall, on an escalator, wearing jeans.

Ooh-La-La

Hi, I'm Mr. Right. Someone Said
You Were Looking for Me?

Crisis:
Breakups

It was Memorial Day weekend 1989, and at twenty years old, I had just moved back to New York after living in Stuart, Florida, where I had been helping my grandmother and her latest husband, Grandpa #3. Here's my diary entry from January 1989:

> I keep moving. I've moved down to Florida and have been here since Saturday. A family call, you might say. Oma is very ill, so I'm here doing what I can. I've got nowhere else to go.

Grandpa #3 had recently undergone bypass surgery, and I'd moved in with them to help out with housekeeping, errands, and anything else they needed. I was happy to relocate again and reinvent myself once more. In between cleaning, shopping, and taking them to doctor's appointments, I got a job waitressing at a casual alligator-themed restaurant in the nearby beach community. Even though I wasn't quite twenty-one, I had an excellent fake ID, so it was easy for me to socialize after work at the local hotspot, which was *the* place to go as the New York Mets baseball team did their spring training only thirty minutes away in Port St. Lucie, and it was a convenient spot for the players to blow off a little steam. Everyone knew when they'd arrive because some of the baseball players would come in and quickly attract the attention of both men and women, all clamoring to get autographs or just take the opportunity to say hello to their favorite player. I didn't know much about baseball, and I didn't care to, so I hung out with my friends from work. We'd sit at the bar and enjoy the baseball celebrity show.

Because I went there so regularly, I quickly got to know and be friends with the cocktail waitresses and bartenders. But there was one particular bartender who went out of his way to sweep me off my feet. He was funny, attentive, and charming. He gave me lots of one-on-one attention and worked hard to make me feel special. He wooed me with an abundance of romantic, silly handwritten notes and showered me with expensive dinners, adorable teddy bears, and weekend trips. He had connections at Disney World, and we toured a section of Downtown Disney (Pleasure Island), now known as Disney Springs, a month before all the nightclubs, shops, and restaurants were open to the public. I thought it was the coolest thing ever. I was utterly taken in by all the attention and was swept off my feet. Our relationship had gone from zero to the speed of light in such a short period that I was dizzy and giddy—and thinking that it was all too good to be true. I should have paid attention to it, but I didn't.

Near the end of May, almost five months into our romantic relationship, he told me he'd gotten a call from his ex-girlfriend; she was six months pregnant.

On the same day that my Disney princess romance story came to a screeching halt, Joe, my #3 grandpa, passed away from his medical complications. Before his death, he had requested that his body be returned to his family for a military funeral at Saint Peter's Cemetery in Poughkeepsie, New York. Within seventy-two hours I had quit my job, packed my car, and returned to New York for good.

Being back in New York meant I was physically removed from the now ex-boyfriend, but I was still in the middle of emotional chaos and heartbreak. Shortly after my return, the phone rang. It was Debbie, my friend since we were three years old. "Get dressed; we're going to the mall. No arguments. Retail therapy is always one of the top best therapies." As all true girlfriends know, a little distraction can go a long way in healing hurts. So, on a rainy late May afternoon, off to the mall we went.

Don't judge a book by its cover.

Even though Debbie was trying to lift my spirits, I was still a teary-eyed, sulking mess. I can't imagine I was much fun to hang out with. Still, she stuck with me as we went from one store to the next. As we were approaching the escalator to go up, she started waving at two guys who were coming down. "Hey, Marc!" Debbie said with a big smile. "Sorry I didn't get back to you." The two of them bantered back, and casual apologies were exchanged. Then introductions were made, and I learned their names were Marc and Carl and that Marc worked as a crane operator for Bill, Debbie's stepfather. Marc reached out and shook my hand, while Carl just kept smiling and nodding. I tried to avoid eye contact because I was a puffy, red-eyed, splotchy-skinned mess, but I couldn't help myself. I noticed how Marc smiled when he talked and how his dimples grew as his smile widened. Even his brown eyes smiled when he spoke. The four of us ultimately said our goodbyes, and I quickly went back to sulking and lamenting the loss of Prince Charming and nursing my broken heart.

At that moment, the last thing I was looking for was a relationship—heck, I didn't even want to go on a date—but something happened that day at the mall that has stayed with me. Sure, Marc was a good-looking college guy, tall and handsome with dark hair, but he wasn't my type. My ideal guy was at least four years older and a little full of himself, and usually lied. Plus, I seemed to be drawn to guys who had issues. Marc did not look or act like someone with issues. On top of that, he was my age, which made him "young" in my eyes as I had been supporting myself since I was sixteen, putting myself through college one class at a time. I thought I was wise in the ways of the world. I thought I was so mature. Yeah, I know how that sounds now. Maybe I was mature for twenty, but I was still just twenty years old.

A month later, I turned twenty-one for real this time, and my friends took me out for my first legal drink. We were all having a great time when Debbie waved to someone over my shoulder. I turned around to look, and there he was, Marc, with his dimples, his smile, and his sidekick Carl. Marc was a nice guy, but I was sure he had to be a ladies' man, a smooth operator, and that he used that smile and those dimples on everyone he met—including Debbie. Though he didn't, I convinced myself that he had a thing for her. In my eyes and my mind, Marc was looking less and less like my lying, deep issues type every time our paths crossed, which seemed to be pretty often. Still, I was uninterested in him.

Needless to say, I was a bit surprised and annoyed when Debbie said she had given Marc my phone number. She thought we should go out together, just the two of us. "He's smart," she said trying to convince me why it was a good idea. "Don't let the mullet and the gold chain fool you. He works hard for my stepdad, and he still goes to college full time."

"I don't know, Deb. He's such a flirt. I'm not really ready to see anyone."

Debbie insisted, "He talks to everyone because he's friendly! I'm telling you, he's a nice guy!"

Hmm, I thought. It sounded intriguing, but I wasn't convinced.

Then she demanded, "Would you just go out with him?!"

A few nights later on a Tuesday, Marc called me at home. We talked for quite a while. On the phone, he was unable to distract me with that smile, but his persuasive charm ended up convincing me to go out on a date with him that Friday night. We did indeed go out, and I was glad we had. Marc was smart. Marc was kind. Marc was confident. He really was the hardworking college guy Debbie had described.

Marc never wooed me—ours wasn't a whirlwind romance of expensive gifts and fancy dinners—but I very quickly realized that he was my friend. He understood me. He was a person I could easily talk to, and we'd talk for hours. He listened to me, and I loved listening to him.

The night of that first date was Friday, August 11, 1989. We went out on that date and have been together ever since. It's hard to believe, but yes, we have been a couple ever since. My friend Debbie was right. I didn't want to believe it, and I didn't want to believe her, but I'm glad I trusted her opinion. Sometimes your best friends know what's better for you than you do.

Here's My Take

Trust can be hard, but we need to trust our friends, our really good friends, the friends who have our best interests at heart. Developing trust with a new friend takes time. It's a process. So often we can be fooled by extravagant gestures, shiny objects, or illusions that turn out to be nothing but smoke and mirrors. If your gut tells you it's too good to be true, it probably is. When a good person is in your life, it feels right. It's easy. It's honest. It's full of long talks and comfortable silences. Not everyone you meet is going to be Mr. or Ms. Right, but you'll never know unless you let that person in and take some time to get to know them, to see them for who they are. Don't dismiss an opportunity merely because it doesn't fit the image you have set for yourself.

The guy whom I thought was too good to be true was. The guy whom I thought was not my type turned out to be exactly what I needed and wanted. If you spend enough quality time with a person, their true colors will show, their personality will emerge, and you'll figure out if you're with a real prince or a total frog. When people show you who they are, believe them.

There's no doubt that a broken heart can hurt like hell, but a broken heart can turn into a crisis if you focus too long on the negative and your loss. Trust your gut. Feel the pain. Grow from it. You will find someone who likes you, loves you, for all the quirky, unusual, and unique characteristics that make you unbelievably and wonderfully you. Don't settle for anything else. In case no one has told you, you are worth it.

What's Your Take?

Do you give people a chance to get close to you, or do you keep people at a distance? Do you find that you quickly judge and dismiss someone because they're not a particular type or because you think they aren't the right person for you? Looks aren't everything, but how they make you feel is. Think about why you react and respond the way you do. You could be missing out on a terrific friend, a great opportunity, or a lifetime companion.

Take It or Leave It

Write down the values and traits of your best friend. This can be a person who is currently in your life, or a best friend from years gone by, or even a best friend you *want* to have. The list can be as long or as short as you'd like it to be. It's your list! Then ask yourself, "Am I embodying these traits?" Remember, your vibe attracts your tribe. This works not only with significant others but also with friends. If you want to attract caring, thoughtful people into your life, you need to be a caring, thoughtful person with yourself and others. The same holds for any other values and traits, be it motivation, creativity, compassion, positivity, encouragement, understanding, or acceptance—and the list goes on. Be the friend you want to have. Be the spouse you want to have. Hold close those people who align with your core values and traits, and consider walking away from those who don't. We all need to believe we are loved and supported in order to grow.

You never know what can grow … in nine months.

Oopsy

The Best and Worst Things Happen Unexpectedly

Crisis:
A Diagnosis

Marc and I hit it off magically on our very first date. There was something so genuine about him that I had not found in a boyfriend before. When he spoke to me, he'd look right into my eyes, and I knew he could see the real me that sometimes hid behind the person I showed the world. When I was with Marc, he made me feel that I could be myself and that being myself was a good thing. He was so easy to talk to, so easy to open my heart to, so easy to show my flaws and scars to. He and I would have dates where we'd talk for hours and hours. We had so much we wanted to say to each other. I was hooked when, on our first date, we talked for hours and hours about the 1987 movie *Angel Heart*, dissecting the movie and the acting, and debating the plot, the symbolism, and what we thought the director's viewpoint was. We'd talk about plans for world travel and exotic adventures. While we never talked about marriage or kids, I think we both assumed it would be down the road at some point. After all, we were still young and under the impression that the world was ours to make. While we were making plans of our own, God was busy making other plans for us as a couple.

November 10, 1990. That was the day that Marc and I found out that I was pregnant.

Oopsy!

We hadn't planned for this to happen, but those two pink lines on the pregnancy kit confirmed that our lives were about to change—fast. We both decided we weren't going to call the pregnancy "an accident" because we both believed that an accident is something you wouldn't do again if given a chance. So we decided to call it "a surprise." Our surprise was due to arrive in July of 1991.

The pregnancy did come as a surprise since I had been taking birth control pills. However, during a routine gynecological exam, I'd been told that my blood pressure was elevated and that I needed to switch to a different oral contraceptive prescription. Around the same time, I also got a bad cold and was taking a course of antibiotics. Without understanding the possible consequences, I was switching over to a new prescription while taking antibiotics and having sex without secondary protection. In hindsight, that was probably not the best combination for avoiding pregnancy, but what happened, happened. After the initial surprise wore off, we started to get excited about our new future: parenthood. While we were working on figuring out the new direction for our lives, baby Eric was on his way into ours.

Our first parental decision was to get married. We picked January 12, 1991, because wedding costs were considerably less expensive right after the holiday and the reception hall we wanted was available at a price we could afford. I'll be honest: there weren't very many people who thought our marriage would last. A few people even had bets; they were giving us five years at best. I can't say I fault them for their doubt. After all, I was twenty-two and pregnant, and Marc and I had only been together for eighteen months. Our figurative "shotgun wedding" wasn't exactly what fairy-tale dreams are made of but, rather, was the foundation for an inevitably disastrous breakup. Still, we decided it was what we wanted to do, and on that day we both said "I do" even if we weren't quite sure what that meant or what we were getting ourselves into.

Standing at the altar on that snowy January day, we both looked straight into each other's eyes and promised we'd stay together for better or for worse. But let's be honest, we all just want the "for better" part. Marc and I were no different. We said the words about being together in sickness and in health, but at our age and in our minds, sickness was something that came down the road when you were old. It seemed so natural to promise all those vows because standing there, looking at each other, life and love seemed so simple. We had no idea how quickly we would be tested. And let me tell you, we were held accountable to every word we pledged to each other on that day.

Our plans involved having an easy, loving marriage with a healthy baby due in July. While we were making plans to support that plan, God was preparing something else. In July, within twenty-four hours of Eric's birth, we were tested with our first vow: in sickness and in health. Not our health, but the health of our brand-new baby boy. At twenty-two, we only had the vaguest notion that marriage vows took work, lots of work. We were about to get a work assignment that would keep us busy for nearly three decades.

> Courage knows what not to fear.
>
> —Plato

I could tell you the story about what happened on that day—I've told it hundreds of times—but instead, I'm going to share with you the words I wrote in my first book, *Beyond Breathing*. Here is the story about the first day of Eric's life and the life that was to come for our family:

> It's positive.
>
> My whole life I had always thought *positive* was a good word. *Webster's Dictionary* defines it as "favorable." And when seven doctors at Westchester Medical Center walked into my newborn son's neonatal ICU room and told me that Eric had tested positive, my first reaction was, "Great! Now let me take him home."
>
> Slow down, not so fast.
>
> Eric was born with meconium ileus, a blockage in the intestines that usually comes out during childbirth. His

didn't. I was still recovering from having him at Vassar Brothers Hospital when I was asked by the doctor on call to pick either Albany Medical Center or Westchester Medical Center because Eric needed to be flown to one of them immediately. I looked at Marc, who looked back at me and then at the anxious, waiting physician, and blurted out, "Westchester."

Two people in red flight suits walked in and put Eric in a small, clear box called an isolate with wires hooked up to him. They whisked Eric off to a waiting helicopter.

I discharged myself, and Marc and I drove by car to meet Eric at Westchester Medical Center, which was over an hour away. He was already in the neonatal intensive care unit (NICU) by the time we arrived. They ran tests for two days, trying to figure out what was wrong with my baby boy. Finally, they had one more test to give him: a sweat test.

Marc and I were in our sterile yellow garments in the NICU. I was rocking Eric in the rocking chair, staring at him. His tiny hand grasped my pinky. He was swaddled in the hospital blanket, which did a poor job of hiding all the wires that were attached to him.

Dr. Doom, the only woman of the seven doctors who had trooped in, reached for my hand when she said that Eric had tested positive. Still, it didn't compute. "The tests are positive. Your child has cystic fibrosis."

Marc looked at me and then at the solemn faces of the rest of doctors. That is when I realized that positive is not always a good thing. Eric had tested positive for cystic fibrosis, and that was not a good thing.

Cystic fibrosis (CF) was unknown to me—a new mom who had just given birth three days ago. What was CF? How did Eric get CF? How can we get rid of CF? Is CF bad? One sentence from Dr. Doom would sum it all up for me: "CF is a fatal genetic disease."

I certainly understood those words. For the next three hours, the seven doctors went on to explain everything we never wanted to know about CF. They told us that cystic fibrosis is a genetic disease that affects the lungs and digestive tract. They said to us that CF causes the body to produce thick mucus that clogs the airways, enabling bacteria to grow, which often leads to life-threatening lung damage. What a nice way to say *death*. They told us that the mucus exists throughout the body, causing the pancreas, reproductive organs, and sometimes the liver not to function to full capacity. They tried to ease our fear by telling us that the pancreatic issue can be controlled with oral enzyme supplements, but they added that, unfortunately, 70 percent of all people with cystic fibrosis eventually get cystic fibrosis–related diabetes (CFRD).

Breathe, I told myself. *Breathe.*

The doctors started getting more detailed and explained that Marc and I were unknowing genetic carriers of the CF gene found in chromosome seven. We'd had a 25 percent chance of having a child with CF. Back in 1989, scientists had isolated the cystic fibrosis gene, and they are now working on gene therapy and, ultimately, the cure for the disease.

The doctors had my full, undivided attention when they disclosed to us that Eric's life expectancy was nineteen years. I was twenty-two. Marc and I had fallen in love with Eric the moment he was born.

Nineteen months later, Eric's little sister, Jena, was born on March 13, 1993. Just six pounds and twelve ounces, Jena too was diagnosed with that fatal genetic disease cystic fibrosis. We had two kids, both with CF, and there was still no cure.

Here's My Take

With some surprises that enter your life, you can choose how to see them, how to define them, and how to work with them. I have found that the words you tell yourself are vital to your overall mental fortitude. Words are important, and the words you tell yourself, or your child, are essential to everyone's mental well-being. I like words, and I'm a writer, so I believe words have the power to motivate and keep you positive and on track. My son was the best *surprise* I'd ever had. He may have been unplanned, but God makes no accidents. Of that I am sure.

It's normal to feel guilt, shame, shock, fear, resentment, isolation, denial, helplessness, and anger upon hearing unwelcome news or receiving a diagnosis of a life-changing illness. The secondary response is a question you need to ask yourself: *How am I going to deal with it?* Our first response when Eric was diagnosed with cystic fibrosis was to close off the world and not let anyone in. We were going to keep the news to ourselves. We didn't want anyone to treat him differently, and quite honestly, we were afraid of how we would handle his future. We were going to lie low until we had a grip on what this new diagnosis of cystic fibrosis meant. After ten days of silence, we realized that a life of hiding the truth wasn't going to work for us. We opened up, we started searching, and in time we found other families who had children with cystic fibrosis. We learned from them and discovered that there was strength in numbers, power in prayer, and at times solutions to our never-ending questions. We reached out and kept reaching out. We still do.

A diagnosis can become a crisis. It is so easy to be defined by what you or your loved ones are diagnosed with. I have always felt that if I let CF define my children or me, the disease has won. My #1 job was to try my best not to live in fear and to work as hard as I could to give my children the best quality of life possible. Trying to accomplish that job was a high-wire balancing act, a high wire that I teetered on every day. And truth be told, I'm afraid of heights.

What's Your Take?

Is there something in your life you felt was easy at first, only to find out how difficult the challenge was? Has there been a time when you talked yourself into or out of something by the words you repeated in your mind? What have you learned from either challenge? Have you ever considered how important the words and your self-talk is to your mental and emotional well-being?

What is your reaction when you are hit with unexpected news and it's not good? How do you deal with it initially? How do you deal with it in the long term? Do you have a support group? family? Do you turn inward and not share your fears with anyone? Is your coping mechanism healthy? What emotions come to the surface?

Take It or Leave It

Fear can be debilitating and can set you on a downward spiral you may not be able to recover from. Dissect your fear. Look at it in the eye and try to figure out what is going on. Sometimes fear is so big that you have no idea how you are ever going to survive. Someone once asked me how I would go about eating an elephant. After the literal visualization raced through my mind and I shuddered at the thought of doing such a thing, the person quickly answered their rhetorical question: "One bite at a time."

Yeah, okay, I've heard that advice before when trying to overcome a large hurdle, but I didn't quite get it at the time. The "one bite at a time" story, however, became clear one night while I was watching *Friends* in Eric's hospital room. In the episode, Ross was about to marry someone, and he froze. "I can't do it," he said.

Chandler, his friend, said, "Well, can you put on your pants?"

Yes, he could do that. So he did.

"Can you put on your shirt?"

Yes, he could do that, so he did.

"Can you walk out this door?" was another question asked.

"Yes, I can do that," he replied, and he did.

And that is how you eat the elephant of fear: you get dressed and you head out that door every single day. You just need to accomplish one step at a time. Nothing is out of reach, even though it may appear so at times. When you are frozen, it's an excellent opportunity to stop and breathe. You've made it this far in life, and you can do it. Fear isn't the problem. How you react to it is. Remember that just taking a breath is a step.

Do these five quick daily mental exercises to keep yourself positive and reduce fear. Answer these in the morning, at night before you go to sleep, or anytime you need a little extra strength to take that next step:

1) Who makes you smile?
2) What are you grateful for?
3) Where is the place that brings you peace and tranquility?
4) Why are you in your marriage, in your career, or doing what you are doing? What's your why that keeps you going?
5) How can you keep that positive feeling going today?

Remember, words matter. What you tell yourself repeatedly in your head is your sincere guide. You're your own life coach. Be a good, positive coach to yourself, and you'll see the difference it makes.

Small changes make a big difference. I hope you'll join me in the next chapter, where I tell you about the Oma principle and where I learn that a small change can lead to transatlantic flights.

Oma Principle

Crisis:
Broke

If you can dream it, you can do it.

—Walt Disney

Supporting myself and having been an emancipated minor since I was sixteen years old, I'd learned to live lean. I'd made it through college on TAP (New York State Tuition Assistance Program) and Pell Grants (federally funded tuition support to those in need) since my income as a waitress and bartender was below the poverty level. Except for the monthly child support payments I received from my dad until I was eighteen, I couldn't count on anyone but myself for paying the bills.

In 1985, when I was a full-time student, I rented a room for $350 a month from my then boyfriend's mother. I wasn't too proud to pick up spare change lying on the ground, and I routinely looked under seat cushions for money left behind. The loose change added up fast and helped pay for the gas that got me to work and school. I didn't budget back then; I was always broke and there was never enough money, so why bother? Being a waitress wasn't an easy job, but it was one I could do. If I had a good tip day, I was riding high, but if the tips were bad, well, it just made life a little bit more challenging. The best thing about being a waitress, though, was that while I worked, I could snack on dinner rolls, olives, cheese, and whatever the soup of the day was—for free. I could afford free. I liked free.

My budgeting mentality changed when my son, Eric, was born. As a young married mom of twenty-two, I learned very quickly that I needed to plan for a future while living today. I needed to learn how to budget, and I needed to learn fast. There was so much more at stake now than just me.

In July of 1991 when Eric was diagnosed with cystic fibrosis (CF), they told us his median life expectancy would be nineteen years and that specialized medical treatment and at-home care would be necessary throughout his lifetime. Marc and I then made the decision that I wouldn't go back to work so I could provide the care Eric needed. Becoming a stay-at-home mom wasn't an easy decision to make. When Eric was born, our combined income was $18,000, and we were already in significant financial debt because we lacked full-coverage insurance and Eric had needed emergency medical care during his first few weeks of life. We slowly slipped deeper into debt with each passing month.

Thankfully, the CF care center where Eric's doctors were located provided us with free samples of the medication that he needed to help get us started. Those samples helped us immensely during the first year of his life. Between me not bringing in an income, our only having one car, and our having a child whose health-care costs were more expensive than Marc's salary, we struggled to make ends meet. But we were young and naive. Looking back, I'm glad we were. We had each other, and we had one mind-set: *We've got this.*

Married life, family life, and all the responsibilities were overwhelming, but we had no other choice. Marc worked fourteen-hour days during the week at Merrill Lynch as a financial advisor, and he continued to work weekends as a crane operator, a job he'd held throughout college, for extra income. I stayed home in our seven-hundred-square-foot, four-hundred-dollar-a-month bungalow caring for Eric and learning all I could about cystic fibrosis. The cottage was so small that in our tiny bathroom, you could sit on the toilet and with one hand touch the sink, with the other hand reach into the shower, and with your feet shut the door.

When I was a child, my parents were always fighting about money. I told Marc we had to work out a financial system we could both agree on because I was never going to fight about money. And I was never going to put myself in a situation where I had to ask him for money either, not for one dollar. Together we worked on our budget. Being a financial advisor, Marc came up with a solid plan we could both agree on. He was adamant about maxing out our 40l(k) and saving for our future, but that left us with very little money to pay for everything else. We agreed that I would get a monthly paycheck of what was left over, and from that amount I would have to figure out a way to pay our monthly bills.

In 1991, there was always more month than money. Funny how that works. It seemed like every month I needed to find new ways to tighten our financial belt even more. During those times, I often thought of my grandmother Oma Eva. She was the queen of being frugal, yet she lived a life of travel, elegance, and style. I needed to become like my grandmother if we were going to survive.

Oma had immigrated to the United States from Germany after War World II. She was a single mother with my then seven-year-old mother in tow and two dollars in her pocket when they arrived in New York City. She spoke very little English, but she had a tremendous work ethic and even bigger dreams. She explained to me once about her Traum Kutsche (dream coach). That was the name she gave to all the dreams she had for the future. Her Traum Kutsche were aspiring yet attainable goals she wanted to achieve. For instance, she told me her first Traum Kutsche occurred the day she saw a plane fly over Berlin. She set her sights on doing the same. Somehow she would find a way and earn a seat on a flight and soar over the city of Berlin. To her, that was like reaching for the stars.

When she emigrated to the United States, she worked at a restaurant bussing tables. In time, she went on to be the owner of a diner. She had high regard for those who worked hard for an honest living and had disdain for those who took handouts. She had pride in all she accomplished and had acquired. Through years of hard work and saving, she made that Traum Kutsche flight over Berlin. She'd made her dream come true. Then she did it again and again, each time to remind herself that she could make her dreams come true with work and perseverance. She spent her hard-earned money on travel, elegant linens, and quality clothes. She never bought anything she didn't need. Any food leftovers she had were frozen as they could be eaten later or made into soup. There was never, ever any waste. She taught me how to reuse, cut corners, and sacrifice well before recycling and DIY became fashionable. Oma knew how to save, and she knew when to spend. I paid attention to her actions and did everything I could in order have more money than month.

As a young, financially strapped married couple, Marc and I enlisted the Oma principle to make our money last longer each month. I would cut napkins in half, I would reuse any paper towel that wasn't too stained, and I'd buy European Selective shampoo and conditioner at Jamesway department store when it was on sale, three for a dollar. I'd pour half the bottle into another container and save it for later, and then water down the remainder of product in each to extend its use. Marc and I shared one car and refused to buy anything that wasn't absolutely necessary. With the special needs of Eric, his care was our most significant and more important expense. For Eric, we never compromised his care. For us, we cut corners everywhere. Marc and I ate leftovers from my mother-in-law's weekly Sunday dinner and generic brand macaroni and cheese during the week, twenty-five cents a box. We promised not to spend anything that wasn't necessary so that we could take care of what we had and try to save. We knew our dream was to eventually buy property and build a house. This became a matter of even greater urgency when I discovered I was pregnant with our second child.

After Jena was born, she shared the closet-sized bedroom with Eric, where there was barely enough room for both her crib and his toddler bed. Marc and I knew we'd have to work at the Oma principle even more if we were going to have enough space for our growing family. When we eventually moved into our own house, I was proud to see that the only money we had spent on our tiny rented bungalow in the three years we'd lived there was three dollars to replace a torn shower curtain liner.

Even though we enlisted the Oma principle to save money, there was another side, and that was to make sure there was joy in our life as well. Somehow, despite all our cutting corners, we still figured out ways to take small family trips and make time for each other. We decided early on not to spend money on little things we didn't need, to fix the things we did have, and never to fight about money. To this day, we have never fought once about money, and that accomplishment is important to me on so many levels.

Fast-forward to 2014. I came home to discover that the glass door on my twenty-plus-year-old stove had shattered into a million pieces. My first thought? *Yay! Now I finally can get that new stove I want!* Nope, not so fast. Marc found a replacement glass door for our model that was only $35 and proceeded to replace the door because the oven was still working fine. Then in 2017, after Eric married and officially moved out of the house, Marc and I decided to have some home renovations done, and I was able to convince my husband we should buy new kitchen appliances even though the ones we had still worked. He agreed, and our stove, refrigerator, and dishwasher went to a family who could put them to good use. They were grateful, and I was excited about finally picking out new ones. I doubt I'll be getting any new appliances for the rest of my life, but that's okay with me.

Love is about fixing the broken things, not replacing them.

Here's My Take

Never give up your dreams. What's the cool stuff you dream of doing? Does it include traveling to exotic places like New Zealand, Africa, or Europe? What about a weeklong romantic vacation on a beach? Taking a family trip to Disney World? Looking at the *Mona Lisa* in France? Visiting the ancient ruins in Greece? Do you want to research your ancestry and connect with distant relatives around the globe? The world holds so many fantastic opportunities that it's a shame how a $6-a-day latte habit could keep you from an incredible adventure.

Here's a thought to ponder: If you can save $10 a day by not going out to lunch, or avoiding impulse items at the store, or going with no-name instead of buying brand-name items, in a year you could put that $3,650 toward that new car you've been eying. or that trip you've had your heart set on but don't have the money for. It's all about goals and your dream coach.

I'm very fortunate in that I had a grandmother who explained to me how I could stretch a dollar so that one day I'd have the money to do what I dreamed of doing. My grandmother always told me that once you attain your Traum Kutsche, you have to go out and establish another one right away. "Life without dreams is death," she'd say. Don't worry, Oma; I'll never stop dreaming.

What's Your Take?

Is there something out there, a dream, a goal, a future, that you're trying to attain? Let your mind wander. Get excited about something to look forward to. Now comes the hard part: Are you disciplined enough to achieve it? Are you doing all you can to work toward that goal, or are you letting that dream move farther away, thinking it's beyond your grasp? What small adjustments can you make today that can get you well on your way to that dream coach?

Take It or Leave It

Grab your notebook and keep track of everything, and I mean *everything*, that you spend your money on in one day. Include the stops for coffee, the candy bar you grabbed when in line at the grocery store checkout, and that shirt or pair of shoes you didn't need but got an email coupon for. Once you've done that, extend the record keeping to last a full week, and then a full month. You'll be surprised. You can now have an answer to "I have no idea where all my money goes."

I've made that list a few times over the past thirty years, and I have always been amazed by what I was spending money on. That helped me to uncover where I could easily cut corners and save cash.

Lastly, being married to a finance guy all these years, I'd be remiss if I didn't remind you to save and save early. If you don't know about compound interest, you should google it. It works. Pennies do add up to dollars, and dollars add up to a future, and your future can support you in your later years. And remember, you don't need to go it alone. Look for a savings support group through your local library, community center, or house of worship. If none are available, look online or start one yourself! You'll be motivated to save when you're surrounded by like minded people.

Turn the page and learn how I tried to save those pennies to buy a future—my son's.

Crisis: Stepping Out of a Comfort Zone

Believe you can, and you're halfway there.
> —Theodore Roosevelt

It was in March of 1992, not quite a year after Eric was diagnosed with cystic fibrosis, that I decided I wanted to raise money and awareness for the Cystic Fibrosis Foundation (CFF). Even though I was a young mom, I had quickly developed a good grasp of his daily routine, his long list of medications, and what his diagnosis meant. With any extra time I had, I wanted to do all I could to help save my son. At the time when Eric was born, the doctors told me his life expectancy was nineteen years. As Marc and I were only twenty-two years old, that pronouncement was flat-out unacceptable. It was also the fuel I needed to bust out of my comfort zone and call the local CFF chapter in New York about volunteering. The woman who answered my call was kind and welcoming. Her voice was confident, yet her words conveyed that she understood the emotions of a new mother whose child has just been diagnosed with this fatal genetic disease. As I would come to learn, she too was a CF mom and, like me, wanted to do everything she could to save her child's life.

At the end of our conversation, the woman said she'd send me a fund raising kit in the mail that would provide me with all I needed to know about fund-raising for the upcoming event she was working on. She told me her name was Doris and that I should call her back if I had any questions once it arrived.

A few days later, I received the package. Eagerly walking back from the mailbox, I tore open the large official CFF envelope and excitedly pulled out the materials. I couldn't wait to pore through them and start making a difference. Then I noticed that the blue folder in my hands had a label on it: "Golf Event."

Admittedly, my heart sank a bit. I was not a golfer, and while Marc knew how to play, he rarely did because he was working two jobs and had little free time. Still, I wanted to do what we could to support the Cystic Fibrosis Foundation, so I opened up the folder. The breakdown of the list of participation and sponsorship opportunities shocked me.

1) Individual golfer—$1,200
2) Foursome team—$5,000
3) Sponsor a hole—$2,500
4) Flat donation suggestion—$500–$1,000

My jaw dropped, my mouth hung open, and I cried. I so desperately wanted to do something, anything, to help find a cure for CF, but even the lowest level was entirely out of our price range. I was clearly out of my league here. They wanted $1,200 to play golf? That wasn't going to happen on our budget! Our annual income was $18,000, and most of our friends were either still in college or riding in the same financial boat we were in—the broke boat. Who on earth would pay for that much money to play golf? Who had that kind of money? Not us.

I called Doris back, but it wasn't long before my composure fell apart and the tears started. "You may think I live in an affluent area, but I'm twenty-two, and we are far from affluent. We live on one income, and everyone I know is either in the same boat or worse," I cried. "I just want to do something that can help save my son's life!"

"Oh, honey," she replied. Her voice now soothing yet still self-assured. "I understand." There was silence on the phone, and then she said, "What about this? Instead of the golf event, can you ask your friends and family for five dollars each?" She paused, and I thought to myself that it was a much more reasonable request.

"Yes, I can do that," I said, sniffling.

"Good, then do that," she said. "We have an event called Great Strides, and it's a walk-a-thon in Rye, New York, on May 10. Sign up as a walker, and bring the money then."

"But that's Mother's Day," I protested.

Without missing a beat, she replied, "What better way to spend your Mother's Day than walking to save your child's life?" She added, "I'll see you there." And with that, she ended the call.

May 10 arrived, and I nervously walked toward the large Cystic Fibrosis Great Strides Walk banner that hung in the entranceway at Rye Playland in Rye, New York. Marc was pushing Eric in a stroller, and Marc's college friend Mike joined us with his eighteen-month-old son Mikey. Collectively, we had raised a total of $750. We approached the walker registration table and signed in, and then we handed our money to the woman with short red hair sitting behind the table. She looked up and gave me a broad smile. "Margarete?" she asked.

"Yes." I smiled back. "Doris?"

She immediately jumped to her feet and came around to hug me. "Happy Mother's Day," she said with excitement.

Doris was older than I'd expected when talking with her on the phone. Even standing in front of her, I had assumed she was in her forties. I would come to find out she was in her early sixties and that her daughter Annie, who was living with cystic fibrosis, was thirty-eight. I remember being amazed by her energy and confidence. She ran the walk-a-thon like a tight ship. Everything and everyone worked seamlessly together. The speakers' speeches tore at my heart, the music playing over the loudspeakers got the crowd pumped up, and the large group of families and friends who came out to raise money and awareness for cystic fibrosis blew my mind, especially on Mother's Day.

The one sentence Doris told me that day that I will never forget was that people don't give to a disease, they give to people. She said those words to me often, and she was so right. Doris instilled hope in me for the future of my child and saw in me the courage I didn't think I had.

Doris wasn't just a CF mom; Doris was a true visionary. Doris Tulcin was instrumental in creating the Cystic Fibrosis Foundation back in 1955 shortly after her daughter Annie was born. Doris never once gave up hope and never once slowed down, doing all she could to save her child's life. Throughout her life, she shed light where once there was only darkness. She was my light and my mentor and will forever be my true American idol.

What I learned through our first Great Strides Walk was that not only could I ask my friends for $5, but also I could educate them about what Eric's medical condition and what our daily life was like. I could explain what cystic fibrosis was based on my firsthand experiences. Doris would say, "Share what you know. That's all people need to hear." She'd say that because CF is such a devastating disease that merely sharing your day-to-day experiences has the power to touch hearts and get people to donate. Doris was right about so many things. I would learn so much from her over the next few decades.

When I called Doris that first day and asked what I could do, she sent me information on the event she was working on. When she realized that the high-end golf event was far out of reach for our family, she gave me something I could do that was within our grasp. Doris gave me a way *in*, and she gave me what I had asked for. I needed something to do that would help save my child's life. Over the years, Doris often asked me to help the foundation in ways that were outside my comfort zone, but I never said no to her requests or to the requests from the Cystic Fibrosis Foundation. She knew what I was capable of doing, and even though I was afraid or feeling insecure, I did it. Doris pushed me out of my comfort zone so I could achieve what my heart wanted me to do. She pushed me past fear and into a world where I wanted to go. I wanted to make a difference, and Doris, and the Cystic Fibrosis Foundation, gave me a path through which to do it.

One of the best compliments I have ever received was at a CFF national conference. As I was sitting next to Doris, she reached for my hand and held it in hers. She looked at me and said, "You remind me so much of me." Doris was not a person who gave compliments lightly, so those words were by far one of the greatest treasures that I would continue to hold dear. Thank you, Doris. I'm forever grateful to you for so many things: the push you gave me, the hope you instilled in a frightened young mom, and mostly your friendship when I needed it the most.

> A ship is always safe at the shore—but that is not what it is built for.
>
> —Albert Einstein

Here's My Take

We all know the first step is the hardest. It requires the most energy and the greatest effort to take that first step. It is also the most fearful of steps. It's scary. We'd all rather stay where it's safe. But after you make that first step, the second step is going to feel a little more natural, and by the third, you have momentum going for you. Your motion is going to propel you forward. Keep it going. The one scary step I took more than twenty-seven years ago was to pick up that phone and make a call. That decision changed the direction of my life forever. Not only have I walked in every Great Strides Walk since 1992, but also I have chaired many CF fund-raising events, have been on numerous committees, and have taken my volunteering and advocacy to the national level. All these things came about because I took that first step. Through my efforts, I have raised millions of dollars for the Cystic Fibrosis Foundation, and it all started with one phone call.

One step leads to many. Consistent baby steps are always the best ones to take. Keep stepping, my friend. Don't stop until you get to where you are going. Get out of that comfort zone that you're clinging to. You may think you need to stay where you are in order to feel safe, but you don't. You can step out, grow, and move forward. Some say life begins the minute you step out of your comfort zone, and I tend to agree. Keep taking those scary first steps until your very last breath, and then your final exhale will be filled with the most fantastic sense of accomplishment of a purposeful life well lived.

What's Your Take?

What is one thing you can think of in your life right now that feels out of reach? Does it feel out of reach because it's out of your comfort zone? Is fear holding you back from doing something you're passionate about? What's one thing could you do, just one thing, that would start you on the journey to where you want to be?

Take It or Leave It

What one step could you take right now to go in the direction you want? Whom could you call? What letter could you write? What text could you send? What one effort can you make? Write down any and all ideas. Maybe you want to take a walk around the block to get more exercise. Maybe you want to give Meatless Monday a try to improve your diet. Maybe you want to submit your résumé for a job at a company you've been eying. Maybe you want to call your local college so you can finally get that degree.

Commit to the person you want to be, but don't think about the steps for too long. If you engage in too much thinking, you'll convince yourself not to take action. The day is here. Do it. Go ahead. Try it. See how far you can go with one step.

If you do one thing every day to get closer to your goal, in one month you'll be shocked at what you've accomplished. One step. Take it and then look back in one month, two months, six months, a year. It will blow your mind how far you went. People often overestimate what they can do in a month and hugely underestimate what they can accomplish in a year. If you take one step at a time, then things you thought were out of your reach will be comfortably within your grasp.

But be careful what you wish for, because you might just get it! Once upon a time, I wished for a large family.

Outlaws, In-Laws, and a Big Italian Family

Be Careful What You Wish for, and Be Thankful for What You Have

Crisis:
Fitting In

Have you seen the movie *My Big Fat Greek Wedding*? If you haven't, you should. You'd get a sense of the family I married into. The Cassalina family might be Italian instead of Greek, but the premise still applies. And what about the now syndicated TV sitcom *Everyone Loves Raymond*? Are you familiar with that one? Change Raymond to Marc, and that would offer you a glimpse into my married life. You see, I live between *all* my in-laws. My sister-in-law lives to the right of me, and my mother and father-in-law live on the left. To add to that, there are over thirty-five of Marc's relatives who live within a one-mile radius of us, and a hundred or so others within the perimeter of our small town. I think you're getting the picture. A super-tight-knit kind of Italian family … and me.

As a kid, I'd sit in front of the TV and watch *The Brady Bunch*. I loved watching their sizable blended family tackle life together, laugh together, go on vacation together, and wrap up everything with a pretty bow within thirty minutes. I'd often feel envious of their big family, and secretly I prayed I could jump into my TV screen and join their adventures. My family life was a far cry from *The Brady Bunch*.

My twelve-year-old self had no idea that sometimes what you wish for *can* come true. So be careful with what you're putting into those hopes and dreams, kids; they just might come back and surprise you!

The day came when I met Marc's family. Even though he has just one sister, the country road they grew up on had, at one point, forty-seven relatives living there. Yup. In less than a one-mile radius on one road in upstate New York, I was surrounded by dozens of well-meaning in-laws.

In 1994, Marc and I built our two-story house next to my in-laws'. The following spring, Marc's uncle Joe rode over on his 1960s farm tractor and dug up a considerable section of my backyard. I ran outside with Eric and Jena in tow and asked, "What on earth are you doing?"

He hollered over the sounds of his tractor and said, "Getting you ready for your garden!"

Flabbergasted, I yelled back, "But I don't garden!"

He smirked, looked down at the freshly dug dirt, and said matter-of-factly, "You do now!"

And I did.

For the next twenty years, I had a beautiful vegetable and herb garden. I planted, weeded, and harvested everything Uncle Joe required I plant. Tending to it all made me feel like a part of the family, a big Italian family. I had rows and rows of tomatoes, zucchini, eggplants, string beans, lettuce, corn—you name it, and it was growing in my garden. I learned how to grow parsley, basil, and chives and to plant marigolds to keep the bugs away. That garden and my green thumbs were well supervised by well-meaning weekly inspections from Uncle Joe and various other family members. With each successful and bountiful harvest, I felt a bit more connected to the extended family whom I loved dearly. I never even minded the thoughtful suggestions on how big my garden should be and how I should prepare my tomatoes to make better gravy (spaghetti sauce) for pasta. It was always said loudly with love.

Another bonus of living close to family was the instant neighborhood watch I got free of charge and without choice. "The Road," as we call the one-mile stretch of neighboring relatives, has better security surveillance than any system anyone could buy. My young family and I were well protected with observant and curious eyes. No one ever drove up or down the road without the entire family knowing about it. One time, a girlfriend came over to visit. She drove a brown van. It wasn't long before I got a call from Marc's aunt, who wanted to make sure I was okay. She had noticed, merely by accident of course, that there was a brown van parked in my driveway that she had never seen before. I explained I was fine and said that I appreciated the fortuity of her concern. To this day, I never worry about our house when we're away, as I know family members on the road will be watching it with eagle eyes and have intimidating shotguns on hand used strictly for hunting deer, rabbits, or squirrels. And even though Marc and I have a sophisticated home alarm system, I still sleep better at night knowing I have protective and loving neighbors who are my relatives whom I could reach out to in an instant for help at any time of the night or day.

Before I married Marc, I never knew families like his existed outside a Hollywood script. I didn't realize families could stay married for generations, didn't realize families could be loud and argue but still stay together. And I certainly didn't know there were so many different types of tomatoes. Sheesh! Everything they did, and still do, is out of love, and that is evident. It's what they know, their culture, how they live as a big Italian family. And they welcomed this mutt of Irish German heritage with open arms.

After being a daughter-in-law for twenty-six years, I became a mother-in-law. My son, Eric, married Kourtney, the love of his life, and I said goodbye to my role of being the one responsible for him. Though I will always be there should he need me, he and his wife are now one union, and I'm confident they will move forward through life's joys and challenges just as Marc and I did. That is the vow they made to each other at Saint Mary's Church on May 27, 2017. They belong to each other, to have and to hold all the days of their lives. During the mother–son dance at their wedding, I was a bawling mess, replaying my little boy's life before my eyes. It was then that I said goodbye to that part of my life and hello to the new Mr. and Mrs. Cassalina, anxiously awaiting the next stage of both our lives. Hands down, it was the best day of my life.

I've been a daughter-in-law myself for almost thirty years, and if my experiences living on "The Road" have taught me anything, it's how to be a supportive mother-in-law. Even though I tried to be more like Marc's family, I came with my own attributes. I didn't do so well trying to match their Italian heritage cooking, but I eventually learned that what I brought to the table was welcomed with open arms. This has taught me that my daughter-in-law is not me and that she brings her special attributes to our family. Kourtney is better than anything I could have wished. She's super smart, she's ridiculously funny in her own unique way, and she can make the best gluten-free apple pie I have ever tasted. She loves my son to pieces, and he absolutely adores her. As a mother-in-law I truly could not be happier.

What I learned from being a part of this incredible family is that you have to embrace old traditions as you make room for new ones. It took time to get used to all the love and affection that came at every turn. Every hello was met with a hug and a quick kiss on the cheek. Every goodbye was followed by another hug, a kiss, and the words "I love you," even if the person had seen me earlier that day. I didn't grow up this way, so all this affection took some getting used to. My family didn't express love with words, hugs, or kisses; somehow you were just supposed to know you were loved. Don't get me wrong, I always knew my family loved me, and when they did on that very rare occasion say it, it brought tears to my eyes.

Now when I see Eric and Kourtney, I tell them I love them with every goodbye, and I mean it with all my heart. I'll even text them the words with the little kiss emoji. I want them to always know with my words, actions, and affection how much they mean to me, while still giving them the spacc to figure out their married lives in their way.

Here's My Take

Every family has its own set of traditions, and all families do the best they can with the love they're able to give. Some families prefer to show their love outwardly, while others hold it close to the vest. Still, both kinds of families show their love in their actions, no matter how small.

I love my daughter-in-law more than she'll ever comprehend, and

I'll work at adjusting to the way she feels love, just as my mother-in-law showed me through her words and actions. I'll keep working so that when the day comes when Kourtney becomes a mother-in-law, she thinks I was a good example of a mother-in-law, or so I hope.

I'm a firm believer that a person's actions speaks volumes more than their words. Words can deflect, but action shows the truth. Before Marc and I got married, he once commented that I wasn't very affectionate. I couldn't believe it. "Me?!" I exclaimed. "But I'm the *most* affectionate one in my entire family, and my grandmother even calls me Love Bug! How can you say that?"

What I realized was that with him coming from his place of love, I could seem a bit aloof, perhaps even reserved. I'm not a cold person when it comes to my emotions, but I had learned to express my feelings differently from the way he had been brought up. In time, I learned his currency of love, and he learned mine. He brings me a cup of coffee each morning as an act of love, and I kiss him at every "good morning," every "hello," and each and every "good night."

When people show you who they are, believe them, whether good or bad, in-law or outlaw. If they show you that they love you, and if they act like they love you and treat you like they love you, believe them. They love you. Trust them. Love them. Communication is vital when it comes to expressing love, and the way you are shown love through actions and deeds needs to be recognized and acknowledged. Even if the words or actions are not what you would do or say, or if they seem strange based on your upbringing, accept them and try to see the love that's at the root of it all.

That being said, there is a big however to what I'm saying about love and how it's expressed. A person may say words of love and may even act like they're in love with you, but if they treat you poorly, do not make you feel like an important part of their life, or are always trying to change who you are, then you need to see them for who they are and what their actions represent. Do they make you question your trust? Do they make you question your sanity? Do they blame it on you being too emotional or too needy? Do they try to convince you it's all in your mind? If you've answered yes to any of those questions, then you need to acknowledge that perhaps you may be manipulated by a person who knows you love them and is not reciprocating truth, trust, and loyalty. You need to see who they really are; otherwise, disappointment, hurt, and betrayal will remain the focus of your relationship. When people show you who they are, believe them. Don't make excuses under the disguised "but I love them" umbrella.

What's Your Take?

There are so many ways to express love other than through words or kisses. What does it take to make you feel loved? Is it words? Is it actions? Is it making the other person's favorite meal? Is it kisses with every hello and goodbye?

Take It or Leave It

How do you say "I love you" without words? Do you know your own "love currency" and the love currency of your loved ones? If not, ask them, "What can I do to make sure you know I love you?" You might be surprised at the answer. It makes for great discussion. Try it. I dare you.

Make a list of the small stuff—the small acts of kindness and the small acts of love that you're thankful for. Make another list of small stuff you can do for others. Thoughtfulness and consideration are ingredients of great acts of love. A simple thought to put the other person's feelings and wants ahead of your own can make all the difference in their being felt appreciated and loved.

Spend some quiet time reflecting on forgiveness. This is also an act of love and kindness as forgiving enables both parties to move on in a positive direction. If you're holding on to anger or a grudge, think about why this is so and how holding on to it makes you feel. Are there things you can let go of by forgiving the person and moving on?

And when you move on, don't forget the hand sanitizer. The world is full of germs.

Overprotective or Overbearing?

Hand Sanitizer Is a Gateway Drug of OCD

Crisis: Fear of a Diagnosis

Even before I started writing my first book, *Beyond Breathing*, eleven years ago, I was a person who lived in a world of words and stories. I've always had the ability to entertain myself for hours by tapping into my imagination. Fairy tales, horror stories, romantic comedies—I can make them up all right inside my head.

Back in 1991, when I was twenty-two years old, pregnant, and newly married, I immediately imagined a story of what our lives would be like. The story went something like this: I'll have a beautiful baby boy. We'll name him Eric Anthony. He'll be bright and inquisitive like his mother, and witty and handsome like his father. Once he starts school, he'll be at the top of his class with excellent grades, but he'll also excel in sports and have lots of friends. He'll go to college on a full academic scholarship, marry the love of his life, and have a houseful of children. I'll gladly look forward to becoming a glam-ma, and while I'll be older, I won't be grayer (thank you, L'Oréal). And all of us will live happily ever after.

My extreme optimism may have been the result of those prenatal vitamins I was taking, but I liked the look and sound of this fairy tale, and I played it over and over in my head. In my story, I never once thought of the words *cystic fibrosis*. I had never even heard of this disease until July 1991, when my son, Eric Anthony, was only two days old. That was the day the doctors told me he had tested positive for this fatal genetic disease.

Eric, my beautiful new baby boy, now had been diagnosed with cystic fibrosis. The story I had spent the last nine months telling myself had to change.

So I did what any writer does to a first draft: toss it to the ground and feverishly begin again. The second version of the story went something like this: My beautiful baby boy, I'm going to keep you in a bubble. I'm going to bleach our world so you'll never touch a germ. I'm going to sterilize the house twice a day, three times a day if necessary. I'll drench every single person who comes within breathing distance of you in gallons of Purell sanitizer. I'm going to give up my life and my friends and devote every single minute of every single day to your treatments, food, medication, and doctors, and to battling the insurance company. I'm going to limit who you play with, how you play, and where you play. Put you in one of those McDonald's ball pits? Are you kidding me? Think of the germs, the runny noses, the coughs, the sore throats, the pink eye, and everything else that will surely make you sick. I'm going to cry every time I put you down to sleep because life isn't fair and I live in a constant state of fear. Every single what-if can mean the difference between life and death. I am going to be responsible, and I'm never, ever—and I mean never—letting you out of my sight.

No doubt about it, I was overprotective, overbearing, and inching up the scale of obsessive-compulsive disorder. But wouldn't you be if your child had been diagnosed with a fatal genetic disease?

I became so obsessed with protecting Eric from every single possible contaminate the world had to offer that even my husband began to tread lightly around me. One day he cautiously mentioned that I had sterilized all of Eric's toys, bleached everything I could, and Clorox-wiped the baseboards in the house for the second time that week. He also wondered if it was necessary for me to read and reread every label, searching for any ingredients that might irritate Eric's lungs.

At the time, I took his gentle concerns as a compliment because it meant I was taking Eric's health seriously. But Marc's concerns lingered in my mind. Maybe I was taking everything too seriously? It wasn't long before I found myself back at Barnes and Noble in the self-help section. I picked out a book about obsessive behaviors, sat on the floor, and took the quiz in the first chapter. I was eager to see where I stood.

Q1: Are you overly concerned with contamination brought on by chemicals and dirt?

A: Yes. Eric has cystic fibrosis, so bacteria, dirt, and unknown pathogens are always a concern. They could adversely affect his lungs and ability to breathe.

Q2: Are you overly concerned about keeping objects (such as groceries) in order?

A: Yes, I keep all foods and medicines with the label side out so I can grab them quickly in case of an emergency. Eric also has an anaphylactic allergy to peanuts, so I need to make sure we have a peanut-free environment. I need to routinely check all medications for expiration dates especially the EpiPen, just in case a peanut crosses the threshold of our sterilized house.

Q3: Do you have images of death or horrible events? Do you worry about fire, burglary, spreading an illness?

A: All. The. Time. With CF, I see danger everywhere.

Q4: Are you afraid of losing something valuable?

A: Seriously? This is my child's life we're talking about.

Q5: Are you afraid of harming a loved one because you weren't careful enough?

A: Yup. Every day. My responsibility. My fear.

Q6: Are you excessive with washing your hands, cleaning?

A: Would my raw, irritated, red-rash dermatitis hands be considered examples of excessive washing?

Q7: Do you inspect garbage before it's thrown out? Do you unnecessarily reread directions? Do you examine the body for rashes or signs of illness?

A: Yes. Yes. And yes.

Q8: Do you repeat asking if something was done?

A: I think I ask "Did you take your medicine?" at least a hundred times a day.

Based on this book, it looked like I had OCD, but deep down inside I was okay with that.

Even if I didn't see it at the time, I was living in the middle of a crisis. I was living with a complicated situation where I had to make smart decisions for my child's well-being, but how those decisions were benefiting us wasn't very clear. As life progressed and I raised Eric, and then Jena, under the dark cloud of cystic fibrosis, I saw that my emotions and reactions would escalate when I felt something might threaten them. I wouldn't let Eric go to preschool if other kids had runny noses or coughs. I would go on playdates with him, worried he might ingest a peanut or not be given the proper medication at the appropriate time. I saw fear and danger at every turn. When I felt threatened, I became overprotective. And, yes, those OCD-like behaviors gave me a sense of comfort and control. I couldn't cure Eric, but I could bleach and sterilize and read and organize everything in our lives. I felt powerless otherwise.

Then one day, when Eric was five, I realized that his little eyes had been watching me oh so closely all along. Eric started picking up my habits and obsessions. He would clean up behind *me*. He became intolerant of even the smallest of messes, and he refused to play outside in the dirt. I was trying my best to let Eric live a "normal" life and not be defined by his diagnosis, but all my actions said otherwise. I treated him differently, and he'd picked up on it. I realized I had taken it too far.

Back to the bookstore and the self-help section I went, this time looking for books about raising a healthy and independent child. There were plenty of good books with lots of ideas and suggestions, but changing my behavior was hard. Still, I did it. I loosened up. I made "Let go and let God" my mantra even as I silently worried about other kids' germs and hidden ingredients. Yes, I was still a mother, and medicine had to be taken and avoiding germs was important, but my days of buying bleach in bulk were over. As I changed my behavior, Eric changed his. Thankfully he was a resilient kid, and over the years he's grown up to be a well-adjusted man who tinkers with cars and enjoys being outdoors and socializing with friends. He's done a fabulous job of being responsible for his own life and managing his medical condition.

Here's My Take

Hold on to those fears that protect you. When it comes to snakes, spiders, and dark alleyways, I prefer to steer clear and leave well enough alone. These fears protect me, and over the years they've served me well.

But what about the fears that don't serve you, that actually limit you from living your best life? Can you push past those fears? That kind of fear is good to push through because a whole new world opens up for you on the other side. One fear I had was fear of failing to be fit. I had a fear I just couldn't be fit no matter what I did. It was one excuse after another: genetics, time, pain—you name it. Facing this kind of fear enabled me to undertake months of rigorous training so that I could hike the Grand Canyon, rim to rim, in one day as a fund-raiser for the Cystic Fibrosis Foundation. Once I pushed past that fear and got outside my comfort zone, I found a whole new dimension of what I could do. And would you believe that Marc and I, along with a committed group of CF supporters, now do an "extreme hike" every year? What started as a huge fear has turned into something I look forward to and enjoy. Sure, it's hard and demanding, both physically and emotionally, but I know I can handle it. I left all those excuses where they belong: at the edge of comfort.

Some fears are all in your head, which can manifest and cause serious anxiety. For so many years I was afraid of being embarrassed or humiliated by the smallest of situations. I was so fearful of everything that I limited my world and my opinion of what I was capable of. Some fears served me well, but many others didn't. I'm so thankful for the words of the serenity prayer; it helped me learn the difference between what I could change and what I couldn't.

What's Your Take?

What have your fears helped you avoid? What have they limited? Are they worth keeping? Some fears protect; some hinder. Can you identify the difference? How?

Take It or Leave It

Fold a piece of paper in half. On one side, make a list of your fears. It's your list, so make it as short or as long as you'd like, but try to put at least five items down. Then on the other side of the column write down what those fears have protected you from and what they may have prevented you from experiencing.

Take a look at your list of fears and see which ones could be added to your bucket list of things you want to do. Then get ready to go on an adventure so you can discover your inner strength and some abilities you never knew you had!

In the next chapter I can organize all that for you.

Overwhelmed but Organized

Keep Calm and Make a List

Crisis:
Overwhelmed but Organized

There's organized, and then there's what I call crazy ridiculous over-the-top organized. It should come as no surprise that what I do falls solidly into the second category.

The early warning signs of hyperorganized behavior arose in middle school. Two words sum it up: Trapper Keeper. In case you never had one, the Trapper Keeper was a turbocharged binder with Velcro flaps that I used to hold all my homework, loose-leaf paper, pens, and pencils. They were super cool, at least by 1970s and '80s standards. I never once lost a paper, my class notes, or an assignment throughout my entire school career. It didn't matter where I lived or what school I was going to; the Trapper Keeper helped me to keep it all together.

Fast-forward fifteen years, and I was a mom of two children diagnosed with cystic fibrosis. As much as I loved those Trapper Keepers, I now needed to graduate to an extra-large three-inch, three-ring binder. I needed as much room as possible to organize all the details about prescriptions, the numerous doctor appointments, and any miscellaneous medical and health information. My new organizational structure included multisectional dividers, colored tabs, and a dozen folders to hold additional papers. In those folders, I'd keep separate records for Eric's and Jena's medications divided into vitamins, enzymes, antibiotics, bronchodilators, and miscellaneous prescriptions.

To give you an idea of the amount of paperwork I had to keep track of, consider the fact that my daughter, Jena, had twenty-two separate medicines that she had to take every day. The first and the most crucial pill was taken to digest protein and fats, and it was so essential to her survival that she had to take sixty-four pills of that one medication throughout the day. If keeping track of the paperwork was a full-time job, then ensuring that my children were taking the correct medications at the correct time was a second one—and that job had no vacations or days off.

For each medication, I included start date, end date, results, and any possible reactions. I'd add my copay and then write in the actual cost of the drug: the cost to my insurance company or the price I would have to pay if I needed to buy the prescription outright. I also listed all surgeries and hospitalizations, including dates, duration, medications, dosages, doctors, and outcome, as well as costs, both the ones to our insurer and the ones we had to pay. Keeping these details about pricing and payments was instrumental when I started advocacy work on behalf of the Cystic Fibrosis Foundation, speaking with elected officials and their staff on Capitol Hill. There were many PowerPoint presentations I created over the years that showed exactly what the costs were and why families so desperately needed the government's support and funding. In 2000, when Marc and I started making our annual outreach trips to Washington, DC, our insurance company covered $250,000 in expenses per child per year, with out-of-pocket costs being the first 10 percent of that. As our annual household income was $18,000 the year Eric was born, you don't need to be a math wiz to see how quick and easy it was for us, and other families, to fall behind.

However, it wasn't just for insurance companies and government policymakers that I kept track of these details. I also needed all this information for hospital and medical staff. In the binder, I kept daily track of what each child weighed and their oxygen saturation numbers, because sometimes how they presented in the doctor's office was different from what had been happening at home.

I kept copies of all medical tests and stored them in the binder. As it was the 1990s and medical records were not computerized, there were many times when hospital staff had questions about drugs, doses, or test results that were not readily available in a hospital chart. Voilà! I was a human computer. The papers in my binder could answer all questions. In addition to the fact that the information was useful for answering questions, it also helped save time every time Eric or Jena was admitted. I had pertinent information about their social and medical history that the hospital would need to admit them. I'd hand that, along with a copy of the medications, to the admitting nurse. It's safe to say that the nurses always, and I mean always, appreciated the list, and most would staple it to the chart and then come in to take all the vitals. Instead of using my time to fill out forms, I was able to spend time with my kids and help alleviate their fears of being in the hospital.

I was the first line of defense for my kids, and I took that job seriously. I was going to protect them from as many unnecessary intrusions as I possibly could. I fended off overzealous interns, unnecessary orders to draw blood, and nurses who took vitals at 4:00 a.m. when the attending doctor said that it wasn't necessary to do so. I wasn't surprised when I learned my nickname among the pediatric nurses was "Mom with the Mouth." Yes, I was the mom with the mouth because I took the well-being of my children seriously. Being in the hospital is stressful. It was my job to reduce that stress as much as possible. I felt it was vital to everyone's mental well-being.

Traveling with multiple medications for two kids was also tricky. Too much? Too little? No matter how hard I tried to pack the right amount before we'd leave for vacation, somehow I'd run short of one medication and have too much of something else. In 1995, I taught myself a new Windows program called Excel and figured out how to list all the medications in columns and then create a function that would tell me how many bottles, vials, or syringes to take with me. It took me some time to get it figured out, but once I did, we were smooth sailing. Our family RV had a decal on the back that said, Roughing It Smoothly. And that is what we did.

My mad organizational skills didn't stop there. The calendar that was stored on our computer and in hard copy on the kitchen bulletin board reflected a very busy family of four. Each day was broken down into fifteen-minute increments starting at 5:30 a.m. and ending at 10:00 p.m., and of course it was color coded. No one ever guessed where we were going or what needed to get done. From fund-raising events to baseball games, to after-school activities, to work obligations, to sharing a coffee in the morning with Marc, it was all on the calendar. Family commitments were in yellow, and doctor's appointments were in gray. School activities were orange. Red for me, pink for Jena, blue for Eric, and green for Marc. Even though it's been years since I've had to keep such a detailed schedule, I can still recall at a moment's notice how it was done.

I know all of this may sound nuts to you. Even I can see how crazy it looks. But I was admittedly a control freak. It kept me on time, compliant, and organized. Once something was entered in the calendar, it pretty much was set in stone. All you had to do was check the schedule, and you knew where you had to be, when you had to be there, and for how long. I followed what the day told me to do. Today, Google calendar and Siri play a similar role. And if you must ask, yes, I still like to have categories, and yes, they are all color coded.

⁂

Here's My Take

When things are overwhelming for me and I feel like life is pulling me in a million different directions, it's hard to know which way to go and how to get there. Life is full of responsibilities, and my life has presented me with some pretty big ones that have challenged me to figure out a way to get it all done. If I didn't do the things I needed to do every day, not only would chaos occur, but also I might have put my children's lives at risk. The only way I could keep my feelings from going out of control was to stay vigilantly organized.

I've met other hyperorganized folks like me; you know who you are. My husband, Marc, may think otherwise, but I'm of the mind-set that a clean desk is a clear mind. Once my office and materials are organized,

I can give myself room to wreak havoc or be spontaneous within the structured boundaries. Being overly organized for all these years has worked for me. It enabled our family to take trips and participate in activities all while dealing with a very time-consuming disease such as cystic fibrosis. I say, if it ain't broke, don't fix it.

By this stage in your life, you may have discovered a process that works for you. But our lives change, and as lives change, so do behaviors. If you feel like life is in constant chaos, then maybe it's time to reevaluate your process. It doesn't matter if you're a person with an "organized messy" desk, someone who still loves three-ring binders, someone who considers Siri your personal assistant, or someone who runs by the seat of your pants: finding an organizational process that works for you is essential to making your dreams and goals a reality.

What's Your Take?

Are you organized? Why or why not? Do you ever feel a need to be more organized? Are you someone who has a messy desk but knows exactly where everything is? What works best for you and helps to keep your life sane? List some reasons why your particular structure works for you and what you like and dislike about it.

Take It or Leave It

Getting organized can be time-consuming in the beginning, but once you get through the setup and you start the habit, it's easy-breezy. Here are a few starter tips to organize your days:

1) Write down your appointments, the dates, and anything you need to commit to, and add it to your calendar. It can be a paper planner or an online calendar, but put those details someplace you'll see them throughout the day. This keeps you in check and also frees your mind from having to remember the small details.
2) Make sure everything has a *home*. Declutter your life by figuring out where everything should go. This includes your closets, your

70

desk, and that junk drawer in your kitchen. Keeping these spaces organized will save you time and aggravation the next time you go to look for that stapler, the highlighter, or whatever tool or accessory you need. And it can save you money by not having to buy duplicates.

3) As you're decluttering, work on the premise of "If you don't use it, lose it." If you haven't touched it, worn it, or looked at it in a while, maybe it's time to donate it, give it away, recycle it, or leave it out with the garbage. Not only will this free up space in your living area, but also it'll free up space in your mind. You'd be surprised by how much room old unneeded and unwanted items can take up!

When you lose the clutter, you can now find your voice ...

Oz: Finding Your Voice That's Within

You Can't Find Your Voice if You Don't Use It

Crisis: Being Forced to Find Your Voice

In 1995, we got our first home computer, a secondhand Hewlett-Packard we bought from my sister. For me, the computer was a fantastic tool that would enable me to dial up and enter a new frontier, the World Wide Web. It was such a novelty at the time, and it seemed like everyone was easily accessing and utilizing the internet. But not me. I was having major difficulties. The computer sat on the desk like an oversized paperweight, and I couldn't get it to do anything. Despite being twenty-seven years old and married with two kids, I was terrified to call the help desk and ask for assistance. What if they asked me questions I didn't have answers to? What if they thought I was stupid? I was so afraid of sounding clueless to the person on the other end of the phone that my anxiety would spike when I was just thinking about calling. I could not bear the thought of being humiliated or embarrassed because I didn't know what to do with this contraption that everyone else seemed to easily understand.

I spent the next two weeks completely frustrated by the computer and my lack of understanding of how to use it. Every day when Marc came home from work, he would remind me that everyone else was just as confused about home computers and the internet and that I shouldn't be nervous about calling the help desk. I didn't believe him. Instead, I believed all the mean names and taunting voices I had heard as a child and a teenager. I was a moron. I was lazy. I wasn't smart like my sister. My sister was smart, and I was not. My sister hadn't had a problem with this computer. In fact, she had already bought a newer model and was doing amazingly smart things with it. The only thing I knew how to do well was to clean my plate at every meal. I was confident that everyone saw my faults and weaknesses and that they judged me as lacking.

However, the fact that we had spent so much money on a computer that I wasn't able to use started to bother me. When I could no longer take the aggravation, I picked up the phone and called the HP help desk.

My heart raced. I stuttered as the customer service representative asked me basic questions about the computer. By the end of our conversation, I had learned how to navigate to the World Wide Web and be among the masses surfing the new internet horizon. Though sweating from nerves as I hung up the phone, I was very relieved. I had survived. It might not seem like such a big deal now, but back then it was a huge hurdle to leap over. Learning how to use this new technology, learning how to ask for help even though I was afraid, was a little step on the long road of overcoming my insecurities. On that day, I felt a small sense of accomplishment, and deep down inside I knew I was beginning to venture into a big new world where I could be outspoken and more confident.

These small steps in finding my voice and developing confidence were instrumental when I had to speak up against our health insurance provider. In 1998, Jena needed surgery to insert a feeding tube into her stomach. The insurance company approved the surgeon, the hospital stay, and the supplies that were needed after the operation, but for some bizarre reason, they would not approve the anesthesia or the anesthesiologist. Seriously?! Their decision made no sense, and I knew I had to get it straightened out. I picked up the phone, called the member services number, and explained the situation, but all the member services representative had to say was, "I'm so sorry, but that appears to be all you are covered for, ma'am."

Her response dumbfounded me, and my frustration level continued to grow. I asked her if approving a surgery but not approving anesthesia made sense to her. "I'm sorry, I can't comment on that. It appears your insurance won't cover the anesthesia, ma'am."

In a very small yet shaky voice, I said, "May I please speak to your supervisor?" There was a long pause on the other end, and then a curt "Please hold," followed by the distorted sounds of Muzak.

This time, I was thankful for the wait. As the minutes passed, I took deep, slow breaths, trying to reduce my anxiety level. To alleviate my uneasiness, I grabbed a notebook and started jotting down all the reasons why the insurance company needed to cover the anesthesia. The most pressing reason was that we were already broke. We were always in the process of paying down our uninsured medical expenses that came from having two children with a severe medical condition and only one source of income. We could not afford to have another huge bill added to the ones we already had.

The list went something like this:

1) Broke.
2) Insurance should cover all of my daughter's surgery. It's not elective or cosmetic; she needs this feeding tube to live.
3) B-R-O-K-E.
4) How can you approve the surgeon, the hospital, and the required supplies but not the anesthesiologist? Do you actually expect people to have surgeries without anesthesia?

By the time the supervisor got on the phone, I had my arguments organized and was slightly less anxious. The supervisor looked at our account and quickly apologized for the error. There had been an incorrect code entered into the claim, but she corrected it. The insurance company would allow for the anesthesiologist and the anesthesia. Even though I was prepared to state my case, I never needed to. I hung up the phone feeling a bit shaky but thankful for the outcome.

Since that time, I have slowly faced my fear of being embarrassed by speaking out and speaking up, and no matter how shaky it was, I found that my voice had a little more confidence. Doing that not only helped me deal with computer problems and health insurers but also helped me to speak out on behalf of all those with cystic fibrosis when meeting with congressmen and congresswomen on Capitol Hill. Through the Cystic Fibrosis Foundation, for nearly two decades I have volunteered to help educate elected officials about this devastating disease and urge them to join the Congressional Cystic Fibrosis Foundation Caucus. Comprised of members of both the House and Senate, this bipartisan caucus works to improve the quality of life for children and adults with CF and their families. From discussing the need to allocate funds for research to fighting to preserve affordable health insurance, our annual Washington, DC, outreach trips have given me many opportunities to grow and improve my public speaking skills. Not only do I feel like I'm helping to find a cure for this terrible disease, but also through my voice and our family's story, I have gradually developed into the person my younger self only dreamed of being.

These days, whether I'm talking to a senator or giving a presentation at a pharmaceutical company, or presenting a corporate workshop about work-life balance, I know those days of being embarrassed about talking and appearing ignorant are behind me. It's incredible to discover how much inner strength is available when something critical (in my case, Eric and Jena's well-being) is at stake.

Here's My Take

To know me now, in my fifties, one would be shocked to discover how insecure and shy I used to be. But it's true. Do I still find it a little scary to speak up? Yes, but I do it anyway. My voice might not be as shaky as it was twenty-five years ago, but it's a voice that needs to be heard. Will some people negatively judge me or not be receptive to my thoughts and feelings? Yes, but I speak my passion anyway. Will some people counter my voice with a booming and more intimidating voice? Yes, that happens on occasion too. But every time I'm met with negativity or anger or dismissal, I ask myself what would happen if I didn't speak up. Like the Good Witch said in *The Wizard of Oz*, "Click your shoes, Dorothy; you had the power all along." Now that I know I have the power, I'm going to use it.

What's Your Take?

Is fear holding you back from speaking up about something important to you? What is holding you back? How is this fear limiting you from doing the thing you want to do or from being or becoming the person you want to be? Who would or could you become if you spoke up on your behalf or on the behalf of someone else?

Take It or Leave It

First, you need to identify what you're afraid of. What is it that is keeping you from using your voice? Is it friends, family, coworkers, or people in a community you belong to?

Once you've identified it, ask yourself where the fear came from. When did it start? Does this fear serve you in any way, or is it keeping you from speaking your truth?

Once you can identify what is holding you back, it may be easier than you think to address it or at least put it in its proper place. Sometimes fears appear like mountains, but when we look at them closely, they better resemble molehills.

Make a list of questions you would like to ask or points you would like to convey. This will help you stay focused and calm. Slowly gather your courage by practicing saying these thoughts and ideas out loud. Try to speak slower, in a more relaxed way, and a bit louder than usual. Adding a bit of volume to your voice can ground you and let the person on the other end know that you mean what you say. Say these things out loud to yourself while looking in a mirror. Stand up and look yourself straight in the eye, and you'll be surprised at the confidence coming from you. Once you feel you've had sufficient practice, set up a time to speak with a person you'd like to share these thoughts with. When you're communicating in a calm, organized way, the person on the other end is more apt to listen to what you have to say.

And sometimes silence says it all.

Obliteration

Crisis:
Loss of a Child

Strength isn't about how much you can handle before you break; it's about how much you can handle after you're broken.

Monday, December 4, 2006, 9:57 a.m., is the exact date and time that my world was obliterated. Everything around me changed, and the only things that remained were my name, my face, and the fact that I was still breathing. Every second, every minute after that moment felt as if I were starting over from scratch.

The death of a child is the worst crisis of all because nothing prepares you for it. The first breath I took after my daughter, Jena, took her last made it painfully clear that I didn't want to breathe; I never wanted to breathe again.

But I did breathe. I didn't have a choice. One breath followed another as the minutes turned into hours and the hours turned into days. My life as I had known it ended with Jena's passing, and a new, altered life began.

Through the depths of my grieving and depression, folks kindly mentioned that my son, Eric, needed me and that Marc, my equally heartbroken husband, needed me, but my thoughts were only about Jena and what I had lost. In addition to losing Jena, I had lost myself. My identity was so closely tied to her, her life, and her will to live despite the debilitating conditions cystic fibrosis had imposed upon her. Jena was my book club president, my fashion consultant, and my reality checker, and now she was gone from my life, from this world, forever.

I'll never forget the joyful moment when the doctor who delivered Jena announced her time of birth, and I'll also never forget the horrific moment when another doctor officially announced the time that would go on her death certificate. The second time was one I was not prepared to hear. I had never given up hope that a cure or a medical solution to Jena's failing lungs could be found. Every day of her life was spent entirely living her life, and I thought we were going to have so much more time before we had to put the final date after the dash. The pain and suffering were unlike anything I had ever felt before. My body knew how to breathe, but I had no idea how to live. I shut down. Completely.

Yes, I was still breathing, and I didn't know what to do with that. I was so angry about being alive, and yet I was still alive. For all of Jena's life, fear had dictated how I lived. Every decision I'd made was based on fear—fear of not being a good mother, fear of not doing enough, fear of endangering her, fear of losing her—and then it happened. Every single fear I had came true. I had failed as a mother, I had not been able to protect her, and I had lost her. All of this had come to pass, and there was nothing I could do about it. There was nothing I could fix or change or do over. The finality was crushing, like a heavy weight pressing on my chest. I had to face my fear of breathing and of living without her.

The funny or rather odd thing about fear is that when you face up to it, either willingly or by force, a whole new world opens up to you. You start deciding how you want to see everything around you. Is it an angry, unfriendly world, or is it a loving world? How could this be a loving world if my daughter isn't breathing? How could a flower or a landscape or a piece of art be beautiful when my daughter isn't by my side to see it? In those early days of my life without Jena, the world felt very cruel and cold. How could my daughter have been denied the chance to see her fourteenth birthday?

Nothing cleanses the soul like getting the hell kicked out of you.

—Woody Hayes

As the months passed, a new and painful world emerged. I started to define life differently. I began to see beauty in things as simple as a budding rose and feel heartache in something as routine as a school bus picking up kids on our street. I'd smile at a rainbow, thinking that maybe it was my Jena trying to say hello from heaven, and I'd cry as I walked past the closed door to her bedroom. During this time, I would lie in bed for hours on end, my thoughts going in circles as I questioned everything. One morning after Eric had gone to school and Marc had gone to work, instead of having another breakdown, I started having a breakthrough. I thought to myself, *Jena came from my body, my flesh, and my blood*. Therefore, she was a part of me and would always be a part of me. And if Jena would always be a part of me, then wouldn't I want her to see all the beauty that was in my world? I began to realize that the best way to honor her life, her beautiful, energetic, live-life-to-the-fullest life, was by living mine the same way as she had lived hers. What if I could start to embrace all that she fought so hard to see? What if I tried to live as though I was showing her the world through my eyes? What if I started living again?

If you think that was easy, think again. When I first started down that new path, I was living first and foremost for Jena, but then I started living life for me, too. After a meltdown, which happened very often, I began to think how beautiful it was to witness the world and imagine her spirit right there next to me, smiling through the tears.

As the days and months went on, I took Jena's spirit with me everywhere I went. I also started to see beauty everywhere I looked because I wanted to share that beauty with her, to share the experience with her, to let her know life was still beautiful. In turn, I started embracing life again. I began to get excited about adventures, new challenges, living. The only way out of darkness is to keep walking through it, and in time the light will appear. I am so very thankful that Jena helped guide me to that light.

Here's My Take

God will continue to break your heart until you decide to leave it open. Being that my heart had been shattered into a million pieces, I decided to try to leave it open. I started to understand that isolating myself from those who wanted to help, those who loved me, and those who didn't want me to feel so much pain would only prolong and deepen my sadness. I gradually began to let them in, and they in turn were able to help me move forward through my painful journey.

I believe the death of a child is a crisis that can result in losing sight of the future, losing hope, and losing the promise of tomorrow. Losing a child can send you into a tailspin from which you may never recover. I know this because there were many times when I truly believed I would never recover. Jena had a fierce drive to live, and I chose to adopt her outlook and attitude to strengthen my resolve to face each new day. When I decided to open my heart up so I could share my world with the spirit of Jena, I started to heal.

It's been over thirteen years since that terrible final day, and yes, there are still days when I cry and long for the family I don't have anymore, but I also smile for the family I had and continue to have. I'm thankful for the blessings of having Jena in my life, for the honor of being her mother, and for the gift of my son and my beautiful daughter-in-law, and my loving, supportive husband. The journey I have been on since that day has not been easy, but every day I look for blessings and gifts because I know they will keep me strong, keep me happy and alive. When I find something that brings me joy or tranquility or excitement or surprise, I immediately want to share it. Being able to share this story, and all the stories in *Embracing the Beauty in the Broken*, with you is a gift to me. Your wanting to seek the best part of your life is a gift for you. I truly hope that both of us can share and enjoy the blessings of being here together right now.

What's Your Take?

Are you living with a heart that is shut? Have you closed it for protection? Have you built walls around your emotions to prevent yourself from getting hurt again? Are you feeling isolated or that no one understands? Do you feel like the world is against you? Is your pain causing you to lash out at others? When anger and judgment well up inside, does it temporarily make you feel better? These are all signs that you're hurting deeply. And it's impossible to heal a broken heart by acting like you don't have one.

Take It or Leave It

Grieving and mourning are so very painful that they cut you to the core of who you are. You can't escape the process. You can't avoid the emotions and the journey. This struggle truly is real. Whether you're experiencing the loss of a loved one or you're a friend or family member of someone who is, the best advice I can give is to let love in and keep your loved ones close. And know that there's never, ever any shame or weakness in talking to a professional grief counselor to help you through the dark days and nights. The light is there, and it will appear if you keep moving.

Even if that movement is just one sip at a time, soup truly is good for the soul.

One Sip

Hard Times Reveal True Friends

Crisis:
Mourning

Even though Eric and Jena had the same two genetic mutations (*G542X/ DeltaF508*) that resulted in them being diagnosed with cystic fibrosis, the disease manifested in dramatically different ways in each of them.

Jena's expression of CF was more severe. From 1993 to 2006 she was hospitalized fifteen times. These weren't brief, one- or two-night stays, but rather three to four weeks in the hospital with around-the-clock intravenously administered antibiotics, nutritional supplements, and a rigorous course of physical chest therapy to expel the thick mucus from her lungs. By age five, Jena needed a feeding tube surgically placed in her stomach so she could meet her four-thousand-plus daily caloric requirements. Yes, you read that number correctly. Four thousand calories each day were needed every day because having CF makes it extremely difficult for the body to absorb the fats and nutrients needed to survive and because the number of calories used by the lungs and body just to exist is high. By age eleven, Jena also needed supplemental oxygen to help her breathe, and by the time she turned twelve, her lung function had decreased to 19 percent. In October 2006, Jena was evaluated and accepted for a double lung transplant. All we needed to do was to wait for a suitable organ donor to appear in the donor registry. We prayed it wouldn't be too long.

Despite the heroic efforts of her doctors, suitable lungs were never found for Jena in time, and she "moved up" to heaven on December 4, 2006. We were too late.

Wednesday, December 6, 2006, was the first morning in over a week that I'd awoken in my own house, in my own bed. Since November 28, I had been by Jena's side every minute of every day. First, we were at the Children's Hospital at Westchester Medical Center in New York, doing everything possible to address her collapsing lungs. Within twenty-four hours of being admitted, we were airlifted to the Children's Hospital in Pittsburgh, Pennsylvania, where we'd have a chance of being a recipient of a donor's lungs. However, lungs never arrived, and on Monday, December 4, at 9:57 a.m., my thirteen-year-old daughter took her last breath.

I don't remember the six-hour drive home, and while I've been told that family and friends were waiting for us when we arrived in the driveway, I don't remember who was there. What I do remember is that I didn't want to walk in the house—the house where I would never see Jena again. I remember that quite distinctly. I remember sitting in the car hysterically crying and Marc allowing me a few moments to process what was happening and to find the resolve I needed to step out of the car and walk toward the back door and into the kitchen.

Once I made it into the house, I felt all the love that surrounded me. I hadn't expected that. I saw the faces of so many people who loved our family and were hurting deeply too. I remember that emotion, but I don't remember much about the rest of our first night back home.

A day passed, or maybe it was two. I remember looking out the bedroom window when I opened my eyes. I looked out the window and at the big branch of an old oak tree that was in our front yard. I stared at that branch, and the tree, for hours, unable to lift my head off the pillow. Crumpled wet tissues were everywhere. I heard someone drive up the driveway and walk into the house. Rustling sounds came from the kitchen, but there were no voices. With Eric still sleeping, and with Marc having gone to handle Jena's service the following day, I threw on my bathrobe and went downstairs. It was my friend Tara. She had let herself in and was placing a container of homemade chicken soup in our refrigerator.

"In case you want to have a little something." Her eyes were red and tearing up just looking at me.

I couldn't even answer her, but I nodded and started to cry. She hugged me, and I wept in her arms. We stayed there until I could breathe again. I didn't eat her soup that day or any of the food that poured into our house over the days that followed. I had such a lump in my throat; I couldn't eat. Everyone tried to have me take a bite here and there, but I couldn't swallow anything.

Over the next week, friends and family stopped over to pay their respects and say how sorry they were. And every day Tara would come by. Sometimes she'd bring soup or her famous apple cake, but most of the time she'd just sit next to me and let me cry on her shoulder. She didn't talk or ask me how I was; she knew my heart was broken. She'd let me ramble through my tears or sob in silence. Tara's daily presence fed my body and soul, and I'm forever thankful for her acts of kindness. It takes a strong person, an amazing friend, to support such intense pain, and my pain didn't scare her away.

Before that terrible day, I'd never imagined it could be difficult to eat a bowl of homemade chicken soup, but it was. It took hours, one sip at a time, and then one bite at a time. It was such a slow, painful process, but gradually eating food got a little easier—and life got a little easier too.

Over the years, people have asked me for advice, wondering what they can do for a friend who has just lost a child, a husband, or another loved one. What can they say? What can they do? What's appropriate? What's not? From my own perspective, I can tell you what is better to do and what is best to avoid. First off, you don't have to say anything. Just offering your love and being there provides so much comfort. Trust me, you won't be infringing or overstepping by sending food, flowers, or cards with kind words. Even a heartfelt text can go a long way. When you behave this way, you become the friend who offers "one sip" of healing. Understand that you will never be able to say the perfect words or bring the perfect gift that will heal their grief, but *you* being present for them is the perfect gift. Just come as you are. You may not fully understand the value of your presence, but the kindness you offer by being there is priceless to a person with a broken heart.

That said, being in the presence of grief is not an easy task. Not everyone can be like my friend Tara who was strong enough to simply sit with me and hold me during my darkest moments. During my period of mourning, I did receive comments and bits of advice that were surely well-intentioned but that missed the mark by a wide margin. Being told "If you think this is bad, wait until you lose your spouse" was one of those things. Another was when an attendee at Jena's funeral came up to me with a smile on her face and a jovial demeanor and said, "Margarete, I bet you don't remember me! Take a guess." I can only imagine she was trying to lighten the mood, but still her tone would have been more fitting had we crossed paths at the grocery store. If you know you have a hard time finding the right words to respond to strong emotions, saying little is absolutely okay. Offer a hug, hold the person's hand, and look them in the eye. All you need to say is, "I'm so sorry. I'm here for you."

Here's My Take

Life can be brutal. Grief can rip you to your core and bring you to a place where you don't think you can carry on or where you don't even want to. There are no words you can ever say that will make any part of the grieving hurt less, but what will make someone heal a little bit is your being there. Share the pain. Take some of your friend's pain as they unleash their raw emotions on you, freeing their heart to heal. The peace, comfort, and breath that is provided by your presence is a relief to those who have forgotten how to live or breathe. Be there. Be that gift. Be you. That's all they need.

Sometimes your presence is present enough.

What's Your Take?

What is or was the hardest thing you have ever done? What is or was the one act you did that carried you through? What one act did you do for a friend who was suffering? How did it make you feel? Were you glad you did it?

Take It or Leave It

Are you wondering about the right thing to do when someone is grieving, hurting, or dealing with a very painful situation in their life? Plan on being there. Depending on the person you want to help, start by sending them a text message, an email, or a handwritten card in the mail or giving them a phone call. Reach out with compassion and see where that takes you. Follow up by checking in with them a week, a month, a year, later. Put the date on your calendar to remind yourself to reach out the following year. Anniversaries of a loved one's death are never forgotten by family, and your reaching out will let them know how much you care.

In short:

- Don't know if you should reach out? *Do it.*
- Don't know if it's right? It *is* (but leave the comedy act and friendly advice at the door).
- Don't know if you can be a strong friend? You *can*. Your friend needs you to be.

And sometimes cutting a branch can help you grow.

Oak Tree

Seeds Planted in the Subconscious Mind Can Grow into Conscious Emotions

Crisis: Subconscious Triggers

Since Jena moved up to heaven, I've gradually accepted that I'll never be the person I was before that fateful day. And I'm okay with that because I don't have a choice. If I want my life to go forward, as Jena would want, I have to accept that every day without her is a new day, and I need to make the best of it. Living this way has meant that everything around our house and home has had to take on new and different meanings. Instead of thinking, *Jena loved sitting in the kitchen. Just being in this room makes me sad,* I've trained myself to say instead, "This was Jena's favorite room. I'm going to sit here and think of the good times we had here. And even though I might feel sorrow, I'm going to focus on the love we shared."

Even though changing my thoughts was (and still is) hard work, the outcome is that I am now able to see beauty in almost everything. You know that expression, "beauty is in the eye of the beholder"? That's my motto, because wherever I am and whatever I'm surrounded by, I want to let beauty and love enter my heart. By allowing more of the positive thoughts into my life, I've lost the ability to let mindless, thoughtless, and trivial things bother my soul. I will never again underestimate the value of a moment, a breath, and I fully understand the incredible power of love.

In the months following Jena's passing, I knew I had to move forward, to find a way out of the debilitating grief that marked each day, but I was so lost that it was almost impossible to see the path. Surprisingly, it was Mother Nature who came to my rescue and taught me a valuable lesson.

In the early days of life without my daughter, I spent most of my time in bed, head heavy on my pillow, vacantly looking outside, staring at the big old oak branch that hung in my view. I watched that branch as the season passed from snow and ice to blue skies and small buds. Time was a mystery to me as I mindlessly watched the buds on the branch grow, and I knew that in time they would bloom into large magnificent green leaves that would one day turn yellow, orange, and burnt red. Eventually the leaves would break free from the tree and litter the ground. In no time, I would be faced with the memories of this terrible winter once again.

Mother Nature was teaching me the cycle of life, showing me that spring follows winter but also that summer leads to fall and that in time winter returns. The cycle goes on, and no one can stop it. I realized this firsthand on a late spring day almost five months after Jena's passing when I found myself at the cemetery lost, searching for my child.

That day was the first time I had gone to the cemetery since Jena's funeral. I hadn't felt the need or the desire to visit her there. My heart and mind refused to comprehend that she was anything but alive and well in my heart, and I felt that if only I were to dig down deep enough, I could hold her in my arms. Grieving—especially a mother's grief—is so very personal and despicably cruel. And somehow that grief prompted me to get into the car and drive. And then, before I fully understood what I was doing, I was wandering, alone and confused, through the rows of family names looking for my Jena.

Then, suddenly, I found her.

I had lost my bearings because I was searching for a newly dug mound of brown dirt with a temporary marker. As I walked up and down the impeccable rows of marble headstones, I could see fresh piles of dirt in between spots of perfectly manicured grass. What startled me was that Jena's resting place was no longer a mound of earth; it was now part of the manicured grass. Jena had been here long enough that life was now growing above her. In the time since her burial, the earth had settled, and Mother Nature had moved forward with her work.

I'll admit it: I was resentful. I questioned how nature could move on so effortlessly while my broken heart was still so raw. Mercifully, seasons change; painfully, life moves forward. Mother Nature taught me that. She assured me that after winter, there is always spring. We may choose to close our eyes and refuse to see the new life that comes, but come it does. The grass turns green and starts to grow.

While I was able to accept that time moved forward at the cemetery, the oak branch outside my bedroom window posed a different challenge. As the years moved forward, I continued to be spellbound by that one branch, and it wasn't healthy. The branch would catch my eye, and before long I'd start to feel the dark sadness return. Sometimes I would curl up on the bed with my head on the pillow and gaze out the window, simply staring at the branch, my mind and mood spiraling into depression. All the positive thinking, love, and good memories couldn't release me from the power this simple object had over me. I guess that even though I learned to live in my grief, I never got past looking at this tree and associating it with my depression. When I made this realization, I mentioned it to Marc, and by the next weekend the branch was cut down.

As I looked out the window each day after the branch was removed, Mother Nature seemed to gently laugh as I intentionally looked at the old oak tree, searching my heart for love. I'd look for new buds on other branches and watch as the leaves turned colors. Having that one particular branch and all its painful associations gone allowed me to focus on the beauty of the tree instead of the heartache. Mother Nature seemingly moves with ease as she repeats life's cycle over and over. She is a master at moving forward, and I have become her eager student.

Here's My Take

Once you identify unhealthy triggers or cycles, try to cut them out of your life, or else they will continue to torment you and harden your heart. It could be as simple as a specific video game that was played over and over during times of sadness that triggers a depressed mood months or years after the initial sadness is gone. But it's not always easy to put your finger on the things that became anchored in your subconscious during those trying times. It took me a long time to realize that the tree branch was a trigger. After I learned that lesson, I began to identify other triggers that reminded me of my depression and influenced what I did, looked at, and thought about. Discovering the triggers takes time, and giving them up can be a challenge, but you need to figure them out and let them go.

For me, I still can't get my head and heart to agree that Jena's final resting place is in a cemetery. Since 2006, I've visited her gravesite only six times. I've learned not to torment my soul with unanswerable pain, and I'm comfortable with this decision because I know she is always in my heart wherever I go.

What's Your Take?

Is there something in your life that makes you sad or uncomfortable just by looking at it? Is there a regular habit or activity you have or do that lends itself to a negative feeling? Is there something you regularly do that often leaves you sad or angry?

Take It or Leave It

Next time you feel sad and you're not sure why, ask yourself, *What song did I just hear? Is there a particular scent in the air? Did the sun break through the clouds at such a time that it sent my memory spiraling out of control?*

If you can identify the correlation, write it down. Keep notes, and maybe you'll be able to see a pattern to your triggers and your emotions. The key thing is to pay attention and not allow yourself to operate on autopilot. When you're aware of what's happening in your emotional landscape, and when you're identifying what your triggers are, you can then decide to acknowledge them or remove them. The trigger loses its power over you once you recognize it and then decide how you want to respond to it. Doing this can make all the difference in your growth and recovery.

Life is beautiful, and there's beauty in the broken, but you have to know where to look and how to look at it. If you forget, spend some time with Mother Nature; she'll show you the way. This I know for sure.

Or you can ask a college director of human resources to show it to you.

On-the-Job Training

You Can't Start the Next Chapter if You're Reading the Last One

Crisis: Struggling to Move Forward

Much like when I reached out to the Cystic Fibrosis Foundation when Eric was born, after Jena's passing, I realized that to cope with my grief in a healthy way I needed to do something to help others, to give me a sense of purpose. Reaching out to others and recommitting myself to the CF community was a way to keep me from feeling sorry for myself and my loss. And it forced me to be productive. It gave me a reason to get out of bed and shower. It gave my day structure, and because I had fund-raising and advocacy work to do, I felt less inclined to lie on the couch in self-pity. I was taking a step in the right direction.

Six months into my mourning period, I mentioned to friends and family, somewhat nervously, that I wanted a "real" job that would force me on a regular basis to get up, dressed, and out the door with the rest of the world. In July of 2007, my mother-in-law suggested I apply for an administrative assistant position at Marist College, the school Marc had graduated from many years before. With Eric soon to finish high school, if I succeeded in obtaining the job, I would be able to help contribute to his college education. Seven months after Jena moved up to heaven, I filled out my first job application in seventeen years. I was taking another step in the right direction.

As I was writing my résumé and cover letter, the reality hit that I hadn't worked outside the home in a long, long time. During the seventeen years of being a stay-at-home mom, so much had changed. The internet was no longer a mysterious, confusing place, and Microsoft Office skills were a must-have for the work environment. I had no idea if I could transition from my former role of a mother manager of children with CF to a professional setting. I was confident the college would not hire someone like me, but I kept working on my application regardless.

Once again, Marc calmed my fears by reminding me that all the organizational skills I used to manage the household were the same skills I would need working in an office. He read over my cover letter and added words and phrases like *great fit*, *skilled*, and *efficient*. I double- and triple-checked the answers to every question to make sure my answers were grammatically correct with no spelling errors. And at 11:30 on the night before the deadline, I submitted my job application. I did it, but I didn't have much confidence in my worth to the marketplace. Why would they give someone like me a job when there were undoubtedly many qualified internal candidates? I waited every day for a call, but none came.

Finally, two weeks later, I received a call from the college's director of human resources. He asked if I could come in on Monday to be interviewed by the Dean of Graduate and Adult Enrollment. I closed my eyes, took a breath, and said, "Yes." I knew if I waited for a second longer to answer his request, my fears would talk me out of going. The gentleman on the other end told me he'd see me in his office at 8:30 Monday morning.

Gulp. What should I wear? What should I say? What should I do? The last time I went for a job interview I was twenty-one years old. Now at thirty-eight, I was beyond intimidated. When Monday came, I put on the only pantsuit I owned and walked out of the house. I was nervous, sweaty, and very emotional, but I managed to keep my composure as I walked into the HR office and introduced myself. Before I knew it, the interview was under way.

When the dean asked about my skill set and ability to navigate through the various Microsoft Office programs, I showed him my "brag book." It was my three-inch color-coded binder full of graphs, charts, and lists that represented seventeen years of caring for my children and their medical needs. This binder had everything. There were Excel spreadsheets with functions. There were color-coded weight and oxygen graphs. There were professional letters I had written to insurance companies, and there was even a PowerPoint slideshow chronicling a day in the life of Jena, which I had used during a CF advocacy visit to Washington, DC, and Congress. The dean flipped through the binder's color-coded calendars and commented that he had never seen such organizational skills for home use. I laughed and told him that my husband often said the same.

The interview had been moving along very well, all positive comments and smiles, so I was unprepared for the curveball question: "So, Margarete, why do you want this job?" All my good vibes came to a screeching halt. I stopped smiling. I stopped thinking, and I started crying. Yes, I started crying. Not big gulping sobs, but a slow trickle of tears running down my face. I was mortified and embarrassed. Once again my emotions had gotten the best of me. I took out a tissue, regained my composure, and explained what had happened during the past year, saying that my daughter was no longer living and that I needed to start living my life again. The dean thanked me for my honesty, shook my hand, and said there were many other applicants he still had to interview and that he'd be in touch. I walked across the parking lot to my car and felt like a failure. The interview had been going so well, and then I'd blown it by breaking down on the final question.

That Friday I received a call from the HR office. They said they'd like to offer me the position if I was still interested. They said my "very impressive binder" had set me apart and was the primary reason the dean thought I'd be a good fit for the job.

Wow. My brag book had gotten me my job, and my vulnerability and honest emotion had not disqualified me. Wow.

For the next three years, I was the administrative assistant to the dean, and I used all of the skills I demonstrated in the binder and learned some new ones. Working at Marist was good for me, and having a daily routine helped me immensely. Life was moving along in a positive and, at times, exciting direction. Yet despite all the beautiful things that were coming into my life, I'd still cry every day over not having Jena in my life. She would have loved to hear my stories about the people at work and the new experiences I was having, and I would have loved to share them with her. So I kept writing in my journal, sharing all my thoughts and emotions, hoping my heart and life would transcend to hers.

Pain is not a valid reason for stopping.

After *Beyond Breathing* was published, I started traveling extensively around the country to talk about cystic fibrosis. An independent production company wanted to turn my book into a movie, and I also received offers from corporations to lead workshops and write materials addressing work-life balance. Eventually I could no longer juggle all these competing demands, so I decided to say goodbye to my career at Marist, which had been filled with fond memories and great friends. On my last day in the office, I thought back to that fateful interview day and the tears I had shed when asked the question about why I wanted this job. While I regretted my honest answer at the time, I realized I no longer looked back at that moment with embarrassment. Speaking my truth allowed me to build a bridge from where I had been to where my future was telling me I needed to go.

Here's My Take

The lesson I learned is that skills do transfer. My skill set of learning, growing, and organizing my family transferred into a valuable asset for the office I went to work in. What I learned was not to discount the skills I'd learned as a stay-at-home mother or from any other avenue of my life. I wasn't always able to believe in myself, but others did. Many other people around me knew that I was more than capable and more than dedicated, and I'm forever thankful for their encouragement. Their faith in me helped me to have faith in myself. Those first few months after Jena moved up to heaven were so very painful. Other than filling my days with crying, coffee, and wine, I had forgotten how to live, and I was close to the edge of no longer caring. I'm so thankful I had good people around me to help me let go of the past and move forward into taking my next step.

What's Your Take?

Has there been a job or position you knew you needed to take, if only as a stepping-stone, until you found your real passion, your real purpose? How did you get there? What unique or specialized skill set do you have? How can you transfer that skill set to another opportunity you might be interested in pursuing?

Take It or Leave It

Take a moment and evaluate where you are in your job or your life. Is it where you want to be, or is it a stepping-stone to the next meaningful adventure? Stepping-stones in life are vital to moving forward. They guide you from where you are to the path to your next destination.

What hobbies do you do currently have that can transfer to a business? What skill sets have you learned—programming, sales, organizational skills, taking care of others? All of these are skills that can transfer into gainful employment. Do your best no matter where you are, and who knows the opportunities that will present themselves, the friends you can make, or the growth you can achieve along the way.

Grow while being true to yourself, and remember, there's only one authentic you. My daughter taught me that.

Original

We Were Born to Be Real, Not Perfect

Crisis:
Fearing That the Real You Is Not Good Enough

Original and authentic. Everyone has heard the saying, "Be yourself because everyone else is taken." But how often do we find ourselves taken with everyone else? How are we to know who we are when we are constantly inundated with what to wear, what makeup to use, what backdrop to use when taking selfies? If you don't have a strong sense of who you are, all the "must use" suggestions that come out of social media could undoubtedly result in an identity crisis.

Many years ago while visiting Disney World, Jena and I saw a live theatrical performance on Main Street USA. The main characters were dressed up as over-the-top tourists from New York City and were slowly driving down the street in a large, 1970s-style red convertible. The skit began when the woman in the passenger seat, complete with bright red lipstick, screamed, "Joey! Stop the car! Stop. The. Car!"

Joey, in his white Disney World T-shirt, bright yellow suspenders, and black dress shoes, stopped the car, jumped out, and yelled back to his wife, "Gladys, why do ya always gotta do that to me? You know I'm driving!"

Gladys jumped out of the car, and the show continued on the streets of Disney. They talked about how they were on the vacation of a lifetime and how they mustn't forget to buy souvenirs for little Joey, cousin Joe, their other cousin Joe Jr., the neighbor Jo-Jo, and Father Joseph from Saint Mary's Church before they get back home.

Jena and I, along with hundreds of other onlookers, watched in amusement as the performers continued their over-the-top banter.

"Joey, we *need* to bring presents home," Gladys pleaded.

"Ah, fuhgeddaboudit, Gladys!" he shouted back. "We can get them at the airport. Little tchotchkes are a dime a dozen. And I ain't getting nuthin' for Joe Jr., so just get that thought out of your head!"

"I don't want trinkets, Joey." She huffed. "I don't want tchotchkes, Joey. I need *authentic* souvenirs," she stressed.

Joey shook his head in defiance, and as a last-ditch effort, Gladys walked up and took Joey's hands in hers and squeezed them. "Joey, honey, snooky-wooky-bear, you know I gotta have the real deal—one of a kind, no imitations, actual treasures bought right here. Authentic souvenirs, Joey. Au-then-tic." she stretched out the word for emphasis.

Joey's face softened as he hugged Gladys tightly and said, "You da real deal, Gladys. You are a one-of-a-kind, no imitations, actual treasure ... you're my authentic souvenir."

The crowd laughed and clapped, and soon we all dispersed throughout the park, but in the weeks and months ahead, Jena and I would often joke about the word *authentic*. Anytime we bought something generic, or whenever I tried to shield her from the truth of cystic fibrosis, Jena would lighten the mood and chime in with a thick, over-the-top New York accent: "You know I gotta have the real deal, one of a kind, no imitations. Au-then-tic, Mom. Au-then-tic."

My little girl knew how to get right to the point. She owned her truth, and she slowly taught me how to be authentic too.

And, yes, in case you had to ask, we did buy some authentic souvenirs that day. Well played, Disney. Well played indeed.

Don't trade in your authenticity for someone else's approval.

You might as well face it: your face is what you show the world. You can't scroll through any social media platform without encountering a plethora of selfies Photoshopped to perfection. You can even alter the "real" you a thousand different ways to reflect the amusing and whimsical wonders of your imagination. You can make your eyes appear gigantic, put bunny ears on your head, or make it look like you're standing on the moon or in the middle of a rap concert.

Applying filters and making edits to an image can allow you to have magazine-quality photos without being a professional model. With an adjustment here and a brushstroke there, we're just softening a few frown lines, removing that annoying pimple, or making those teeth just a little whiter and brighter. But when does all that correcting go too far?

It's a slippery slope when you're continually enhancing a picture because you're not content to post the original. Why is that? Are we using the image-manipulation apps so we can get the likes, the comments, and the positive affirmation that our altered self is better than the authentic?

Are we forgetting to put the real us out there anywhere?

I'm the first to raise my hand and say I've used all the available filters. It's fun and silly. I can make my voice sound like a chipmunk, but I can also have my face be perfectly symmetrical with a flawless complexion. I recall the first time I came across these photo editing tools back in 2009, and I quickly became obsessed. In no time, I stopped posting any photos of myself without first fixing anything that I thought was even a little less than perfect, and I would be mortified if friends shared group photos that included me on their social media accounts. My smile wasn't just right. My eyes were half closed. What's going on with my hair?! I was so wrapped up in presenting a "perfect" me that I couldn't see how a friend's photo captured a precious moment of time spent with people who were important to me. Of course, it was only a matter of time before I'd cross paths with online friends, and the realization would set in that how I made myself look online versus what I looked like at the grocery store, or picking up dry-cleaning, or getting gas could be very different. In my real world, not every hair is in place, there are freckles and pimples and age spots, nails get chipped, and I like to wear my son's oversized college sweatshirt. Thankfully it didn't take long before I realized that all of us, myself included, are far more interesting and unique when we show our undeniably beautiful authentic imperfections.

We compare. We contrast. We conform.

All of these social media platforms are here to stay, but where are the limits? I often wonder if all this image altering is having a negative impact on our collective self-esteem. Are we living in a world where our children are growing up having to keep up with everyone, not just a Kardashian? Isn't it up to all of us to embrace the fact that real beauty always starts within? The real you, the raw and real you, is still your best face. Never lose sight of the real you.

But, hey, if it makes you happy to play around with the filter options, go for it. Just don't let the real you get lost in translation. Don't let those "enhancements" change who you are inside.

Here's My Take

We live in a world where so many people want to be, act, and look just like everyone else. Just scroll through the pages of Instagram and Facebook, and you'll see so many identical "duck lips" and "rested bitch face" that it'll make you wonder if we've lost touch with what is real. Each one of us was created to be unique, not to be, look, or act like everyone else.

To quote Disney World's Main Street USA actor, "You da real deal. You are a one-of-a-kind, no imitations, actual treasure. You're this world's authentic souvenir."

Au-then-tic.

What's Your Take?

Have you ever compared your most-disliked physical trait to someone else's trait that you define as perfect? Have you ever changed your looks, your hairstyle, and your wardrobe because you felt pressured to be something other than what you are? Are you afraid the real you isn't good enough for your family, your friends, your job? When you're making these comparisons, do you think you're treating yourself fairly? The bigger question is, how does it make you feel?

Take It or Leave It

Want to try a few filters that you won't find on your smartphone? Brighten up the hue of your heart with blessings. Saturate yourself with kindness. Adjust the love levels from within. Blur the lines of anger. Highlight the good in your life. Fade the negative thoughts. Sharpen the gratitude.

Go ahead, play around with the latest apps and find out what Hollywood celebrity you might look like, but face it, the people who love and care about you would much rather see the real, beautiful you than anything else.

Be-U-tiful!

Moving forward isn't always beautiful or easy, and sometimes you need professional help.

Out of Control

I Jumped Out of My Skin and Just Kept Jumping

Crisis:
Panic Attacks

My first panic attack was on November 29, 2006. The backstory is take from my book *Beyond Breathing*:

> *Just step over me,* I thought.
>
> I just wanted Marc to step over me and leave me there. I was a terrible mother. I was on the floor with no shoes or socks, my hair was wet, and I couldn't move. We were supposed to be on the med flight to Pittsburgh with Jena in forty-five minutes. I had tried to take a shower while Marc stayed with Jena in the PICU with Dr. Boyer, and here I was on the floor at the Ronald McDonald House at Westchester Medical Center.
>
> Since yesterday I hadn't eaten, I hadn't slept, I couldn't stop throwing up, I had diarrhea and a migraine, and my blood pressure was through the roof. And there I lay on the floor as the manager of the Ronald McDonald House

stood at my feet. She had no idea what to do with me and kept reminding me to relax and put my feet up and breathe.

Relax? Breathe?

I should have been with Jena, but I couldn't even sit up. To relax and put my feet up and breathe sounded so ludicrous while my entire world was falling apart, yet it was the only thing I was able to do. I told the nice woman to please call Madelint immediately since she'd know what to do, and I gave her Madelint's number, which I knew by heart.

Madelint was my lifesaver and my friend, and she also happened to be Dr. Boyer's right arm. She was a registered nurse with a master's degree in social work, and over the years I am sure that degree had come in handy more than once in dealing with me. She always popped her head in every time we were in the hospital or at a doctor's appointment; even if it wasn't with Dr. B., she'd be there. She was terrific, and she was the only person who could help me. She would know exactly what to do.

She had been with me all day the day before in the ER while they attempted to reinflate Jena's collapsed lungs. She was there to hold my hand and to be there.

In a matter of minutes, she was beside me again. She brought with her another nurse and Dr. B. They knew what was going on, and they knew I had to be on that plane to Pittsburgh or else I would never be able to live with myself. They all got on the floor with me, checked my temperature, checked my pulse, checked my heart rate, and held my hand. I knew they would take care of me. Dr. B. said I needed Valium, and I would be fine. Even in the state I was in, I didn't think that was such a good idea. The last thing I wanted to be was knocked out. I had to be here for Jena, but I was no good to anyone on the floor.

"Just step over me and take care of Jena!" I cried.

Dr. B. just grinned knowingly and told Madelint to take me through the ER and make it *stat*. He was going back to be with Jena and Marc. They should have just stepped over me, but I owe them everything that they didn't.

Madelint helped me into a wheelchair. I was so dizzy, I didn't know we were already in the ER, where she signed me in, answered all the questions, and asked them to please hurry.

In fifteen minutes I had been diagnosed with severe anxiety, panic attack, and trauma. The ER doctor on call prescribed me five milligrams of Valium with five refill prescriptions. Madelint had explained what was going on with Jena, and he figured I might need more. Unfortunately, both he and Dr. B. were right. Within five minutes of taking the Valium, all my symptoms subsided to a bearable level, I could function again, and my first thought was of Jena.

That was the first of many panic attacks I would have. They continued throughout my recovery from Jena's passing; they continued throughout the two years journaling that eventually ended up as my memoir, *Beyond Breathing*; and they continued throughout the year I traveled around the country speaking to groups about the book and cystic fibrosis. Typically, I would wake up in the middle of the night drenched in sweat with my heart racing. I thought I was doing well trying to figure my life out without Jena, but apparently something in my brain didn't entirely agree, and the panic attacks were supposed to get my attention. They did. And I developed a series of "counterattacks" designed to alleviate them. I started exercising regularly. I put aside time every day for quiet reflection. I improved my diet to cut back on caffeine and sugar. These strategies weren't a miracle cure, but they did help to lessen the severity and frequency of those dreaded encounters.

What finally broke me was not the first time my son, Eric, almost died from a CF-related emergency medical complication, but the *third* time.

It was 2013, and our family, including Marc's parents, who had recently retired, took a trip to Italy. We wanted to see the country and enjoy the sights, bask in the history, and eat some fantastic Italian food. I was looking forward to overloading on gelato in every flavor.

The day after we landed, Eric started having health issues, and by the time we arrived at our Tuscan villa where we were all going to stay, the situation worsened. We called for an ambulance and followed Eric to the local Siena teaching hospital, where his condition quickly escalated into a life-or-death situation. We stayed at the hospital for four days while doctors tried to save his life and get him stabilized so he could be transported back to the United States. Despite struggling against the language barrier between the Italian doctors and his doctors in New York, and despite the massive confusion of being in a foreign country with our critically ill child, we finally got a twenty-four-hour window in which Eric could be evacuated via an ambulance plane back home. We were all fully aware there were no guarantees he'd survive the flight. Every single moment was harrowing and horrifying. Eric used every ounce of his breathing composure and strength to survive the flight.

The plane did land with Eric still hanging on. He was taken by ambulance to his New York hospital, where an entire medical team was on alert and waiting for his arrival. They utilized all measures in record time to save his life. After a considerable amount of time, we eventually got Eric home. While his recovery took several months, he did indeed recover. But during that time, I developed full-blown posttraumatic stress disorder (PTSD). I couldn't handle a quiet moment in my head, and I couldn't handle being startled. A single cough from my son could send my adrenaline soaring and land me right in the middle of a panic attack. I couldn't watch TV except comedies because any suspenseful moment or drama would send my anxiety through the roof. My adrenaline wouldn't stop flowing. My fight-or-flight response mechanism was on overdrive. I couldn't function. All the strategies I had used in the past to ease my panic attacks helped a little, but it wasn't enough, and I began to slip into depression. Every moment of every day, I felt like the fear and suffering would never end. This time I knew I needed help—professional help.

I started with a psychiatrist. She told me I had no control over these episodes and quickly wrote prescriptions for antidepressants and antianxiety medication. I explained that I didn't like taking medication and said I was hoping for behavioral therapy skills I could use instead. I explained how I thought exercise and journaling seemed to help in the past but that I didn't understand why these techniques weren't working so well now. After handing me a ninety-day supply of Zoloft and Xanax, she gave me the phone number of a psychologist but informed me that the therapy more than likely wouldn't work, that I needed the pills to live, and that I would need to see her every three months if I wanted the prescriptions refilled.

When I left the doctor's office that day, I felt like I had just gone to a drug dealer. I wanted to understand what was happening in my mind and body, not just take a pill to "fix my problem." I had the prescriptions in one hand and the number to the psychologist in the other. I went off to the pharmacy, and while I waited for the prescription to be filled, I called the psychologist to make the next available appointment.

In retrospect, I'm thankful for the opportunity to work closely with the psychologist. She listened to me. She gave me action steps. She told me I wasn't crazy and said that if I had the desire to get better, I would. I did. She explained to me how and why my panic attacks had worsened. We made a plan to schedule regular appointments once a week for the next three months.

She suggested I take the medication during that time as it would help me while I worked on my steps for addressing and alleviating the PTSD. She provided me with practical and effective strategies and structures that helped to resolve my issues. Soon I was able to decrease my medication, and my symptoms gradually lessened. With her help, I decided that I didn't want to go back to the psychiatrist and that I didn't need the prescriptions refilled. What I had needed was someone to help me build a bridge from my panicked, confused brain to a place where I could function normally. The psychologist provided me with the coping skills and mechanisms for what I was dealing with. There's no doubt the prescribed medication helped me during that time, and with it I was able to work my way back to myself.

The strong person is the one who asks for help when he or she needs it

Here's My Take

Before Eric's medical emergency in 2013, I had never gone to a mental health professional for help. While I had navigated the pain of Jena's death on my own, Eric's crisis painfully taught me that I couldn't handle everything. I'm embarrassed to admit this, but before that event occurred, I was a person who never thought about going to therapy. I couldn't understand why people didn't just figure out a way to solve their problems. Now that I know firsthand how working with a psychologist and psychiatrist can help, I sincerely apologize for my judgment and my ignorance. Panic attacks are your body's way of letting you know you're stressed beyond control.

In the year that followed, I redoubled my commitment to getting well, and the struggle to do the work was real. Despite my love of sweets, desserts, and all things chocolate, I knew that refined sugar triggered my attacks, so I needed to be very careful to avoid them. I also knew that exercise and running kept my stress levels in check, so I needed to incorporate some of that into daily life—no matter how busy or tired or uninspired I was feeling. The effort paid off though, and I learned so much about myself and what caused the PTSD and panic attacks. I can happily say that I've never felt as good as I do right now.

What's Your Take?

Have you ever had a problem that you felt you couldn't handle by yourself, one for which you knew you needed professional help to address? How did that make you feel? How did the professional assistance help? Did anyone suggest a quick fix that didn't sit well with you? How did you handle that? What was your path, your journey, to get back to health? What is your opinion about therapy?

Take It or Leave It

One of the strategies I still use when I feel like my mind has gone haywire is the 3-2-1 Feel technique. It is quick and it helps to bring my mind back to the present moment. Here's how it works:

Pick three things that you can immediately see, touch, smell, and hear, and name them. Then ask yourself, "How do I feel?" Next, choose two things that you can see, smell, and hear, and name them. Then pick one thing.

For instance, right now I'm sitting in my office. If I felt like a panic attack was approaching, I would stop and take a deep breath then initiate the 3-2-1 technique.

I see ...
1) a picture of my family hanging on the wall
2) a coffee cup
3) a bouquet of roses left over from my twenty-eighth wedding anniversary.

I can touch ...
1) this keyboard
2) the mouse next to the keyboard
3) the lukewarm cup of coffee.

I can hear ...
1) a plane flying outside
2) a car driving by
3) a dog barking off in the distance.

Next is, what do I smell? I take another deep breath.
1) I can smell the coffee.
2) I can smell the perfume of the roses.
3) I can smell the hand cream I just rubbed into my hands.

Then I ask myself, "How do I feel?" I feel ... *calmer.*

I repeat this process, sighting two items each time, then eventually just one, like so:

I *see* a paperclip, I *touch* my iPhone, I *hear* the motor of the computer, and I *smell* the fabric softener from the laundry drying down the hall. I *feel* better.

While doing this, your mind will need to focus on the present and what is currently in front of you. This strategy works well when you find your mind lingering in the painful past or creating fearful future scenarios that have not happened and may never happen. Coming back to the present moment presses a reset button and can help you to avoid triggers that create stress and panic.

But what do you do when you're dealt another diagnosis?

Oncology

My Doctor Asked Me if I Had Ever Had a Stress Test. "Yes," I replied. "It's Called *Life*!"

Crisis:
When Life Gives You a Diagnosis to Worry About

It's 2003, and at thirty-five years old, I'm getting ready for my very first mammogram. Even at that stage in my life, I had already known several women who had had breast cancer, so I knew I had to be diligent and proactive when it came to cancer screenings.

Naked from the waist up, I was squashed, pulled, and poked by a woman in her late sixties with icy-cold hands. When the test was over, she asked me to take a seat back in the waiting room for a moment. One moment turned into twenty minutes, and when she returned, it was with script in hand. She informed me that there was a large mass in my left breast and I needed to come back for a needle biopsy.

"A what?!" I asked.

"A needle biopsy. There's a lump in your breast, and we need to take a piece of the mass to determine if it's cancer or not. Right now, we can't tell."

"Oh. Okay," I said, taking the piece of paper from her hand. "When?"

"Can you come in tomorrow?"

Gulp. *I guess this is serious.*

Through the years of caring for my two children with cystic fibrosis, I knew not to "borrow worry" when a troublesome situation appeared. I had learned that nugget of wisdom from Jena. You'll read about that story in a later chapter.

The next day arrived, and I headed back to the mammography center for the biopsy. I lay down on a paper-covered table in a darkened room and stared at what looked like an x-ray machine. The medical technician said she was going to insert a needlelike contraption into my breast and that it would grab and remove a small piece of the tissue. The whole concept of the needle biopsy was to determine if the mass in my breast was fluid filled, meaning just a benign tumor, or a solid mass that could be cancerous.

The needle made a *pop!* sound, and I felt a pull and a tug. And while the pain was bearable, it was uncomfortable.

"Hmm, I'm not sure I got enough. Gotta go in again," said the technician.

Pop! Another sample.

"Hmm, well, maybe just one more for good measure," she said.

Pop!

As I climbed off the table and put my shirt on, she told me the results should come back shortly. I was okay with that. I was not interested in borrowing any worry just yet.

A few days later, the phone rang. I was told the results had come back as undetermined. I was referred to an oncologist, and she told me the best course of action was to have a surgical procedure called a lumpectomy. She believed the mass in my breast was not cancerous, but because the needle biopsy hadn't shown that conclusively, it was better to be proactive and remove it. I scheduled an appointment for the following week to have the procedure done. I was hoping for the best. The oncologist didn't appear worried, so I was not going to do that work for her.

As a result of the surgery and the final biopsy, it was determined that the mass in my breast was a rather large fibroadenoma, a phyllodes tumor that was benign (good news—not cancer). However, the tumor had "sprouted legs" and attached itself to my breast wall, which had made it appear suspicious and increased the risk of its becoming precancerous. Removing it was the best course of action for the long run.

During the lumpectomy, the doctor removed the mass, but he also scraped out a large section of the breast tissue that surrounded it. Discussions before the surgery suggested I speak with a plastic surgeon as the procedure would result in "the girls" being dramatically lopsided. She was fairly confident it wasn't cancer and said that if I were to make the decision to have an implant placed in the breast that had undergone the lumpectomy to regain its original size, this would be the best time to do it. If it ended up being cancer, then our options would have to wait. Both doctors agreed, and when I woke up from surgery, I didn't have cancer or lopsided girls. The result was that I looked exactly as I had looked before all the talk of lumps and biopsies began. Mission accomplished. My identity was preserved with implants. No need to buy new bras or shirts or anything. Chapter closed. Or so I thought.

Until now. When I turned fifty, I decided it was time to send "the girls" on a farewell tour. What had made me feel comfortable and confident and sexy when I was thirty-five doesn't work for me now. I want the implants out of my body. I know this means I'll need to undergo cosmetic reconstructive surgery and that how I look and what size bra I'll need to wear will be different, but I don't care. I want my body to reflect who I am today, and I want to be comfortable, emotionally and physically, in my own midlife and slightly sagging skin. And the girls, as wonderful as they were at thirty-five, still reflect that thirty-five-year-old bosom. It's time the girls, my skin, and me all get on the same page. "Da real deal. The one-of-a-kind, no imitations, actual treasure—real, authentic, lopsided boobs."

Hopefully, this story is the nudge you need to make sure you're getting regular wellness exams and following through on routine preventative tests like mammograms. While you're making those appointments (if they're not already on your calendar), be sure to schedule one with a dermatologist for a routine skin cancer check.

When I was a kid, I loved being outside in the summer and frequently got sunburns because no one in my family ever used sunscreen. Skin cancer prevention wasn't as known then as it is today. You burned, you peeled, and you dealt with it. It wasn't helpful that when I was a teenager, and well into my thirties, I loved to get as tan as possible, thinking it gave me a healthy glow. Well, those burns from long ago landed me at the dermatologist with questions about odd-shaped marks. Now and for the last several years, I've needed to have at least one superficial basal cell carcinoma (a type of skin cancer) removed from my back and shoulders. This happens often. I now have a standing date with my dermatologist every six months to make sure any cancerous skin cells are quickly identified and removed before they grow into something more serious. Needless to say, my days of tanning beds and lying on a beach doused in baby oil are far behind me. Sunscreen with an SPF of 50 is my BFF and never far from reach.

"Doctor! Doctor! It hurts when I do this!"
"Then don't do that."

In the months after Jena moved up to heaven in 2006, I began having rashes, headaches, and stomachaches. At first I thought it was all part of the grieving process I was going through, but as my emotional state improved with time, the physical symptoms only worsened. Some days it felt like glass was slicing its way through my intestines, and the headaches turned into full-blown migraines that left me unable to do anything but lie down in a dark room, vomiting for days on end. For the next two years, I went to all sorts of doctors to try to figure out was wrong. Gallbladder? Nope. Working just fine. Heart? Nope. My cardiologist was adamant that the hole in my heart was not responsible. Allergies? The allergist thought environmental factors could be causing these problems, so he sent me for further testing and blood work. When the results came back, he informed me that I had three markers indicating a high likelihood of celiac disease. He then added that I also had the signs of being lactose intolerant. No more gluten and no more dairy.

My first reaction was, *"What?* But I love pasta! Carbs are my soul mate! And ice cream in a waffle cone. And cream cheese on my bagel. And butter on my bread. What the heck am I going to eat?"

Sitting in front of the allergist, I was told to focus on a plant and lean protein diet — vegetables, chicken, fish, quinoa and rice, and a little fruit now and then. I was told not to eat any dairy, wheat, rye, or barley for the next six weeks to see how I responded.

"But that's through Thanksgiving *and* Christmas?!"

Let me tell you, I followed the doctor's advice but was a very vocal and angry bitch about it. Marc and the rest of the family can attest to that. It was mid-November, and for the next six weeks I had to give up everything I loved to eat. Thanksgiving through Christmas was 100 percent gluten-free and dairy-free. No apple pies with real whipped cream, no Christmas cookies, no stuffing, no eggnog, no cheesy garlic bread, and no pasta.

I think my Italian mother-in-law felt even worse than I did.

"What? No pasta? No bread? No chicken parmigiana? What are you going to eat, air?"

"No. No. And no. I don't know what I'm going to eat." I huffed.

I was miserable watching everyone else chow down on all my favorite holiday dishes, but my body was starting to feel better, so I knew the allergist wasn't just trying to ruin my holidays. I think. When January rolled around, I had an endoscopy, and it was confirmed: I had celiac disease.

In the ten years since that diagnosis presented itself, I've gotten used to eating differently. And so has my mother-in-law. We've found substitutes for wheat, rye, and barley so that during the holidays I can still enjoy those delicious family recipes. I can occasionally tolerate having cheese or ice cream, but I cannot eat gluten at all. On the very rare instances when I have "cheated," I very quickly paid the price—and I was reminded that the intestinal pain and discomfort is just not worth it.

Here's My Take

As Jena taught me long ago, I try not to worry until I know for sure that there's something to worry about. Worrying is like praying for something bad to happen, and it only lowers your mood. But when a worrisome diagnosis does present itself, it's important to take action to avoid future damage if it's at all possible. For me, it's more important to have a long, healthy future with my family than to be that supertan mother-in-law with big boobs who spends all her time locked in the bathroom because she can't stop eating fettuccine Alfredo with extra cheese.

Long, long ago, before all these various illnesses and diagnoses, I promised Marc I would take care of *myself* for him, and he vowed to take the best care of himself for me. We have so much future ahead of us, and being as healthy as we can is essential so we can enjoy it together.

What's Your Take?

How do you handle an unexpected diagnosis or getting sick? Are you "borrowing worry" before you even know what's wrong? How good are you at following doctor's orders even when the diagnosis is not what you want to hear? Do you have a support system in place to help you follow through?

Take It or Leave It

I have found that the best medicines available are free, like sunshine (with sunscreen!), water, rest, fresh air, exercise, and healthy eating. It's as old as time, but people still don't do it: Make sure you are setting your annual doctors' appointments. Know what you're doing well at and where you need to make improvements. Make the time to take care of yourself before it's too late. You're important to the ones you love and the ones who love you. And that colonoscopy you've been putting off? Call now.

Go and make all those appointments you've been putting off. You'll feel better just for doing it. Really, close this chapter, make the call, then come back, and we'll talk about the time my friend tricked me into meditation. Namaste.

Ohm and Meditation

Meditation: Because Some Questions Can't Be Answered by Google

Crisis: Being Unaware That Stillness Is an Option

The first time I heard the word *meditation* was more than twenty years ago. My friend Cindy called to invite me over to her house for a "guided meditation" she was organizing for a group of women. I told her I'd go, but secretly I wasn't quite sure what I was getting myself into.

When the day came, I showed up at her door dressed in my fuchsia exercise pants and a white cotton T-shirt that said "Namaste" across the chest. I also had brought along my yoga mat to be on the safe side.

"I'm ready!" I said as I walked in the door.

"Um?" Cindy said as she looked at me quizzically.

"What?" I said, starting to feel uncertain.

"We're not doing a workout or stretching. We're going to breathe, balance, and reflect upon our inner selves."

"Oh, right," I said, still having no idea what any of that meant. I left my yoga mat by the door.

We went into the living room, which was dimly lit by a few carefully placed candles. The aroma of lavender and sage filled the air. As I sat on the couch, I immediately thought of those fancy resort hotel spas. *Where's the herbal tea and water with lemon? Where are the fluffy slippers and bathrobe? What time is my massage scheduled for?* I tried not to smile or, worse yet, laugh.

No sooner had this thought crossed my mind when a steaming cup of chamomile tea was put into my hands. I quietly sipped and looked around anxiously as a few more women came in and got settled. Once everyone was comfortably seated, my friend pushed play on the tape deck, and the deeply resonating tones of gongs transitioned into quiet nature sounds of birds and flowing water. The soft-spoken voice of a woman explained how to breathe in deeply, how to exhale, how to center our thoughts, how to clear our minds, and how to become one with ourselves.

So this *is a guided meditation?* I thought. *What a waste of time!* For the thirty minutes that the tape played, these thoughts circled my brain. Sometimes I tried to follow what the soothing voice was telling me, but most of the time I was thinking of all my responsibilities that I had to take care of when I got home. I'd thought I was coming here to do some stretching, some yoga, some Pilates maybe, and instead I was sitting on my butt doing nothing. *Nothing.* I tried to breathe deeply, but I could feel my heart racing with the thoughts going through my head of how annoyed I was that I was sitting here instead of getting things done. I certainly didn't understand any of this talk about "centering" or "being one with yourself." I had no idea where my center was, and I hadn't the slightest idea how to find it.

When it was all over, my friend, who now looked very relaxed and happy, asked me how I liked it.

"Honestly," I said, "I would have rather done yoga. At least I'd have been moving or something."

She chuckled and told me that I should try it again.

"Yeah, maybe," I responded.

In my mind, I was thinking, *Absolutely not!*

But Cindy was persistent, and as a stay-at-home mom with two young kids, I looked forward to a little me time, so the following week we tried it again, and again, and again. As the weeks passed, I continued to struggle. My mind wouldn't calm down because my brain was always adding more things to my mental to-do list. The one time I did manage to finally slow my thoughts down, I promptly fell asleep. I was a meditation failure.

After one of our weekly get-togethers, Cindy handed me a small booklet, *A Beginner's Guide to Meditation.* "Look at this when you're at home, Margarete. It'll only take you ten minutes each morning to do."

I took the booklet from her. I looked at the cover image of a woman, calm, eyes closed, hands clasped, and in deep meditation. I clenched the booklet tightly in my hand, and all of a sudden a wave of anger and frustration came over me. "Cindy, I don't have ten minutes! What I *do* have are two little kids with CF and a ton of stuff that has to be done, and I never have enough hours in the day to do it." I was almost in tears.

She paused.

"Well, then." Her smile grew. "Sounds like you'd better start with two hours of meditation instead."

She may have been exaggerating, but her point was valid. She was warning me that if I didn't stop the high-speed pace of the stressful life I was living, I would be headed for a breakdown or at the very least be rendered unable to handle the psychological sucker punches that parenting children with cystic fibrosis can bring. I still didn't know what my center was or where I could find it, but I knew I needed to keep looking. If I could find it, I knew it would help me get through all the uncertainty and fear in my life.

I used that little booklet a lot. Eventually I was able to find a sense of peace when I sat in bed at the end of the day, closed my eyes, took a deep breath in, held it for a second or two, and then exhaled long and slow. I listened to the air going in. I pictured the air filling my lungs, and then I pictured the same air moving out of my body, washing my tension and stress away. The flow of air was all I focused on for those few minutes, and as I did that, my body relaxed and my thoughts slowed down. Much to my surprise, I discovered that being aware that you are in fact breathing can be a magical tool all on its own.

Have you ever seen a flat tire roll? Probably not. Why? Because it needs air to roll well. And so do you. You need air if you want to roll with life's punches. You need to treat your breath and the air you breathe as a trusted partner. Let it help you so you can help yourself. Seriously. This is coming from a high-stressed, type A personality control freak.

Meditation is so much more than lighting a few scented candles and "focusing on the breath," although that is a great place to start. For me, meditation is about pressing the pause button on a hectic, emotionally charged life and spending time with myself. Slowing down and being still fills me with gratitude for each breath and the blessings in my life and helps me to focus on the good that surrounds me every day.

It took me a long time of practicing meditation before I started to enjoy it for the emotional benefits it brought. In many ways, those early days of meditating weren't all that different from making sure Eric and Jena took their CF medications. I looked at those few minutes of quiet breathing as "taking my meds," and even if I didn't like it, I did it. But I'm glad I developed the habit and stuck with it because meditation became another tool in my toolbox for dealing with our roller-coaster family life.

Perhaps you don't know what spending days on end in a hospital is like, but I do. From the day following my son Eric's birth to the day my daughter, Jena, moved up to heaven, I have been one of the many, many moms and dads who have had to spent days, and even weeks, at a hospital because our children have special needs or a terminal illness. Even if you've never been in a hospital, try to put yourself there for a moment. Try to imagine anxiously sitting in that hospital chair. Try to imagine feeling hopeless and angry while you hold yet another cup of coffee that you don't dare stop drinking because you need to stay alert to deal with the crisis at hand. It's here, in this dark and uncertain place, that finding your breath and a sense of stillness can keep you from plunging into deep despair. In the stillness, you find comfort in knowing that a higher power loves you. You feel the support that comes from family and friends being by your side, and you discover hope in trusting that every medical professional is doing their very best to restore your child, or other loved one, to good health.

Meditation. I'm so glad I didn't hold fast to my initial thoughts that it was a big waste of time, because the long-term return on investment of having a meditation practice was, and still is, worth the time and effort. Invest some of your valuable time by pausing for a few minutes or more every day. Invest time in finding your peace and tranquility; that's how you'll know you've found "the center" (hint, hint).

Here's My Take

At some point in your life, as is true for all of us, life will throw a curveball that will knock you to the ground. I know from experience that this can be true. Sometimes I refer to myself as Humpty Dumpty: shattered, broken, and pieced back together. When I was broken, I searched desperately for peace in my heart, frantically trying to find tranquility. Meditation and stillness seemed impossible. My breath was ragged and choppy with pain and sorrow, but I knew that even during the worst of times when my heart was battered and broken, the light of hope would shine through and guide me to where I needed to be. They say the crack is where the light can enter.

After Jena passed away, I remember looking out the bedroom window in complete misery and despair. I didn't want to be alive. I didn't care about eating, showering, or even breathing, but I was doing those things. And I hated it. After the initial hard-core grief, I started feeling guilty that I was breathing and my daughter was not. How unfair was that? Then, slowly, I began to see the beauty that was gifted me with each breath. I was able to see my husband, the man I loved so very much, every morning, and the touch of his skin eased my pain. I started feeling grateful for the smallest of things that breathing gave me: the opportunity to see my son's smile, to see flowers bloom outside, to hear the laughter of young children at the playground.

Holding on to that light helped me to become grateful for my life and for being alive. Gratitude is so much more than being thankful for the good things and the good times. Gratitude is about appreciating the value in everything that has happened: the good days, the not so good days, and the days that are sheer hell. It's about being grateful for every moment in your life that you survived and every breath you have taken.

Like the breath that moves in and out of my body, the blessed life of the world around me has gone on. I am grateful when I have the opportunity to see my daughter's childhood friends, now all grown up and starting lives of their own. At these get-togethers, I always cry a little, but I also smile and laugh, knowing that Jena's spirit is with them and that she too touched their lives. The hearts of those who loved her greatly will forever hear her.

And when, at the end of the day, I'm feeling cracked and broken, and the pain of loss returns, I come back to my quiet place, my breath, and the stillness so that I can feel the light of hope return. Then, before I fall asleep, I hug my husband a little tighter, knowing that the real love we created began with us. And his presence beside me eases the pain.

What's Your Take?

Do you have a daily meditation or prayer practice? If not, how do you center yourself when your world spins out of control? Do you ever feel unable to be still with your thoughts? Are you worrying about your ability to handle life's ever-changing swings? How can you give yourself the gift of peace and tranquility in your daily life?

Take It or Leave It

Put aside ten minutes of your day to reflect on the blessings in your life and to express gratitude for everything you have, including the parts you don't like or wish would go away.

Pay close attention to the things you are having difficulty expressing gratitude for. Are you holding on to anger, sadness, or grief? Are you giving another person power over your emotions instead of taking full responsibility?

Try to put aside just five to ten minutes each day to be quiet and listen to your breath. When you give yourself time to sit in quiet meditation, reflection, or prayer, that strong person inside of you will emerge, and you'll recognize life's many blessings and the peace that these blessings can bring you. Give thanks for the gift of life that breathing brings to you. If that feels good and you want to do a little more, consider starting a journal by writing down your thoughts along with a gratitude list.

And to get you started, here are a few tools I've personally used that have helped me along my path:

- Apps for your phone—Headspace and Insight Timer (they're free!)
- Journal writing—see Julia Cameron, *Morning Pages: The Artist's Way*, 25th anniversary edition (October 25, 2016)
- Read S. J. Scott and Barrie Davenport, *The 90-Day Gratitude Journal: A Mindful Practice for Lifetime of Happiness* (July 30, 2018)

Write and meditate until that aha moment changes it all.

Oprah's Aha Moment

Crisis:
Being Afraid to Share Your Story

> The more you seek the uncomfortable, the more you will become comfortable.
>
> —Conor McGregor

Fun fact: According to the *Merriam-Webster Dictionary*, the first known use of the phrase "aha moment" was in 1931. But I'd like to think it became an everyday expression thanks to Oprah Winfrey. How many times did we hear her triumphantly bellow on her television show, "Aha! I get it now! Light bulb moment!" before she'd explain the latest insight that would alter her life, and maybe ours, for the better. Thank you, Oprah.

My aha moment came unexpectedly following a surprise turn of events. After Jena moved up to heaven in 2006, I began writing an online journal that collected all my thoughts and memories of her and our family's life together. Marc, true to his nature of always believing in me more than I ever believe in myself, quietly emailed the document to a friend of ours, Frank DeFord, who had lost his eight-year-old daughter Alexandra to cystic fibrosis in 1980.

Frank was more than just a "CF dad." He was a sportscaster and a very prolific writer with eighteen books published and an ABC made-for-TV movie that was based on the story he had written about his daughter, *Alex: The Life of a Child. This* is the person to whom Marc sent my online journal, my deep, dark secret diary, my honest and vulnerable detailed emotions. And I had no idea he had done this until I received an email from Frank.

After the initial shock of realizing what Marc had done wore off, Frank's positive and thoughtful email response validated that the raw, real me had written a story that was worth telling and sharing. "Your story is really lovely and so touching. I found myself crying like a baby so many times, and I actually had to stop and put it down for a while. Jena absolutely comes alive. You write with such feeling. I want to thank you for letting me read it." Frank ended his email by encouraging me to publish the story. My horror at having someone like Frank read my Jena stories abated, and I became thankful that my husband saw value in the words and worth in my emotions put to paper, which I had been hesitant to share beyond our immediate family and very close friends. Frank's message validated my efforts and prompted me to push myself past my fears of being judged and criticized for putting the raw and real me out there. I started taking steps to have the stories published.

It took some time to find the right publisher and prepare the story for publication, but I stuck with it, and my perseverance paid off. Within a year of *Beyond Breathing*'s release in October of 2008, I was awarded the Editor's Choice Award, the Readers' Choice Award, and the Star Award by iUniverse, the publishing company.

My aha moment was that being real matters—the real, raw, and broken but beautiful me matters.

Even though it's been over ten years since the book was published, I still feel awe and appreciation every time I get a letter, an email, or an online comment from someone who has just been introduced to the book and felt compelled to share their story in return. Before I overcame my insecurities about publishing my family's stories, I questioned why anyone would want to read about our life, but when I hear from readers, I see how my story has impacted their lives. I feel as if my broken heart has been carefully picked up and loved by people from around the world.

All those years ago, when I first sat down to write those stories, I wasn't sure if I could heal my broken heart, but I have done so, and every person who has written to me has been a part of that healing process.

I might not have aha moments as frequently as Oprah, but learning to keep it real has changed my life. Most of the time we don't want to show the world our flaws, our failings, and our pain, and instead we try to hide the realities of life behind a veneer of perfection, which is exhausting. In the past, I so desperately wanted people to think I had a normal and in-control life and that nothing, not even the fear and uncertainty of being a parent of two children with CF, would ruffle me. I'd stress over all that. I'd cry over that. I can't tell you how many times a day I'd beat myself up for not being all that I thought the world wanted me to be. I was miserable because I was trying to be everything *but* me.

The raw, real me was someone who often went to bed crying, sometimes hysterically. The raw, real me woke up with puffy, swollen eyes, my nose raw and red from crying, and my face flushed and blotchy. When Marc or the kids would see me in the morning, I'd blame it on allergies and take a Benadryl. What I hadn't yet realized was that the people closest to me saw through all the excuses, saw through all the ways I'd try to keep them from seeing how scared I was. Those people always wanted the raw, real me. And it took the positive words of strangers who read my book to bring that lesson home—literally.

Here's My Take

Keep the curiosity going, and look for new aha moments. They can occur when you open your heart and soul to change. They happen when you are looking for a new way of focusing and expressing yourself. When it happens, you'll know it. Chances are, your mind will stop for a moment, and you might even find yourself saying, "Aha!"

You can go along in life staunchly committed to one way of thinking, but that might not be the healthiest choice. For me, I was deeply committed to the thought that the real me was never good enough. And then, after exposing my raw and real self to the world, I realized that I *am* good enough. My life, my story, *is* good enough. It was a moment when I saw myself in a different light. I became kinder to myself. I became a friend to myself instead of a bully. I gradually stopped all the negative self-talk that would fill my days. That aha was huge.

As Oprah used to say, "Oh, the tiny hairs on my arm just stood up!" Now I chase after those feelings that make my tiny hairs stand up. When that happens, I know I'm headed in the right direction.

What's Your Take?

Have you had an aha moment that changed your world? Did it come unexpectedly? What has changed since? Do you feel lighter? Do you feel more empowered? Do you feel there's more to uncover? What did you learn about yourself that you didn't know before?

Take It or Leave It

You might be wondering how you'll know when an aha moment arrives. In my experience, those little eureka moments are usually found in the quiet times, either through meditation or silent reflection.

You might also want to keep a notepad by your bed. Your brain has a way of releasing insights right before you go to sleep because you're relaxed but not yet off in dreamland. Ask your inner self to work on what you've been struggling with, and maybe you'll be presented with an idea right before you doze off or when you first wake up in the morning. Either way, you'll be glad the notepad was there.

If the time immediately before and after sleeping isn't a good one for you, try writing your thoughts down during a few moments when you do have a bit of quiet time. A journal is very useful in so many ways. It gives your brain and your heart topics to explore. And if you're more artistically inclined, let your pen doodle, draw, or just scribble on a notepad. Whether it's images or words, these daily actions can help stimulate thoughts that are lurking underneath the surface, just waiting to come out. Get into the habit of spending time with your journal, and you'll be surprised by what comes to the surface.

And though you may think you have it figured out, there's no doubt there could be a coup brewing.

Offspring and Obligations

To Keep Your Child Close, You Have to Let Him or Her Go

Crisis: Letting Your Child Take Responsibility

It was a revolt against authority. There was a coup brewing, and I was about to be overthrown. My parental reign was nearing its end. I was no longer in control of my son, and he was reminding me of that at every turn.

I should have known this was coming. When Eric was young, he was eager to be independent, and Marc and I encouraged and supported his desire to be a "little man." As a toddler, he'd get his cereal bowl and spoon from the kid-height bottom drawer and had learned to swallow all his cystic fibrosis medications in a single gulp.

As an elementary school student, Eric would set his alarm for 5:30 a.m. to get up, get dressed, take his meds, and do his breathing treatments. As a preteen, he taught himself how to ride a four-wheeler and a snowmobile and administer his own insulin shots. As a high school student, he started a landscaping business and took sole responsibility for his college applications. Once he had his driver's license, he also began scheduling his monthly pulmonologist appointments.

When he started college, Eric balanced a full-time job at a local bank with a full-time class schedule. And after he turned eighteen, he took over admitting himself to the hospital whenever he needed a more aggressive intervention for a cystic fibrosis flare-up.

In the early days, I was his safety net. I watched him balance his personal life, schoolwork, household responsibilities, and CF, ready to step in at a moment's notice if his decisions started to go wrong. While I loved watching my son soar into his independence, I had a hard time watching him fall. Perhaps he didn't clean his nebulizer as often as I thought he should. Maybe he didn't take his meds at the times I thought were best. And sometimes that independent adolescent attitude got a little hard to handle. Sure, he was growing up, and growing up fast, but as far as I was concerned, he was not all grown up just yet. In high school, he began to show independence, and our conversations sounded like this:

"Don't you think you should see the doctor about your cough [or your sinuses, or your stomach pain]?"

"Ma, I got it," he'd answer, annoyed.

"Did you remember to mention your cough [or your sinuses, or your stomach pain] to the doctor."

Irritated, he would reply, "Ma, I got it."

Next we'd endure a quiet ride home where he repeatedly refused to talk about his conversation with the doctor.

"Don't you think you should do your nebulizer [or take your pills, or test your blood sugar] now?"

Frustrated, he'd reply, "Ma, I got it."

Next he would stalk out of the kitchen and go to his room, slamming the door shut.

"Did you order your antibiotics [or your bronchodilator, or your insulin] from the pharmacy yet?"

Exasperated, he would replay, "Ma, I got it."

Next angry words would be exchanged when I had to run to the pharmacy down the street because Eric hadn't placed his mail-order prescription in time.

"I'll stay with you in the hospital, you know, just in case."

Speaking very directly, he'd respond, "Ma, please go. I got it."

What happened next: tears, lots of tears, and sobs in the car as I drove myself home.

Our mother–son conflicts grew as Eric continued to assert his independence. As I would sit and stew over the latest battle, I acknowledged that he was handling some aspects of growing up very well and responsibly—but I had given everything in my life to take care of his. I was so much better at managing his life than he was. I was a master when it came to organizing, charting, and planning for every little aspect his health, and he was relatively new to being in charge of his life.

And then I had one of those aha moments: It was his life, not mine. It was his health, not mine.

In my head, I could hear Eric's tired voice saying, "Ma, please, don't worry. I got it." I felt lousy. I was turning into the mother I swore I would never be. I didn't want to be the mother who thought her son could do nothing right, who did everything for him, and who reminded him of it at every opportunity. I didn't want to be the mother who nagged and pleaded and tried to manipulate. I didn't want to be the mother whom her son turned away from because he was being suffocated by fear disguised as love.

Damn. This realization hurt, and I knew that what I was going to have to do would be hard. But I had to do something. We had to do something to take this parent–child relationship from "at odds" to "much better." So what did we do?

We discussed boundaries.

We discussed fears.

Each of us discussed our newfound independence.

After I realized the error of my ways and tried to make amends, Eric responded by opening up and sharing more with me. Shortly after he transitioned from pediatric to adult care for cystic fibrosis, he asked if I wanted to take a ride with him to his next doctor's appointment. I sat in the waiting room, and when he was done, he introduced me to his adult care team one at a time. They were terrific. They all said what a wonderful son I had, and I couldn't have been happier to have been invited. These were the medical professionals whom Eric could count on when he needed care, and it was easier for me to relax about his future knowing these people were in his life.

On our way home, he asked if I wanted to get some lunch. Over a ton of sushi, we talked about his life, his job, his girlfriend (who is now his wife), and, yes, his health. It was a positive conversation, full of talking and listening, sharing and laughing. The days of my unchecked fears and his simmering sullenness felt long ago and far away.

When the server brought the check over, I fell into my old habit of reaching for it, but Eric quickly beat me to it and smiled, giving me his best, "Ma, I got it."

Oh yes, Eric's got it for sure, and I couldn't be prouder of the man he has become. My role as Mom has permanently shifted, and it continues to amaze me how all this time went by so quickly. Even at twenty-eight, he's still my little boy. There are times when I look at his face and feel myself being transported back to the days of long ago when he was a young child who loved to hold my hand, kiss me on the cheek, and randomly say, "I love you, Mommy!" Every day, I consider myself blessed to have him in my life.

Being the parent of a child with a fatal genetic disease takes life down a painfully unique path, and it can be frightening to transfer control over to the child with an illness when the time approaches. While our family is waiting for a cure for CF, I have to let my son figure out how he wants to live his life. After all, it is his life, not mine. Just like taking ownership of his education, social life, career, dating, and now marriage, he needs and wants to own his disease and be in charge of his own health-care decisions.

Eric will always be my child, my little boy, and my grown son. He is a part of me, and a part of Marc, that is living and breathing and walking around on this earth. The least I can do, to show him how much I love him, is to let him fully live his life while I fully live mine.

Here's My Take

Outbursts are a sign that your child is trying to be independent. Your child is trying to figure out who he or she is and where he or she fits in the world around him or her. Deep in your heart, you know you have to let your child go. You must give your children independence. Yes, it's not easy, and yes, it's easier to do everything for them, but if you continue to do that, they'll never know how to do it for themselves. You give love by teaching them how to be the best capable adults they can be. I once read that it's easier to raise a strong child than to fix a weak adult. Children need to figure out how to pick themselves up after they fall, they need to know what it feels like to hurt, and they need to know how to rely on themselves. You figured out how to be a grown-up through trial and error, so let them do the same. They need to experience their life, and you don't need to live your life *and* theirs.

One of the best pieces of advice I've received was to love the child even if his or her behavior is breaking your heart and keeping you up at night. Know that behind every temper tantrum meltdown, every slammed door, and every sarcastic comment, your precious child is trying to figure out how to walk, talk, and relate to his or her changing life. You are there to give your children solid roots while they learn how to fly.

What's Your Take?

What has been your biggest challenge in dealing with your child's or children's independence? What things did you do well that made a significant impact on your relationship? Is there something you're still working on? Adolescence is a hard stage to go through on both sides. Is your sweet little cherub face now spewing backtalk at you? Is your child keeping secrets? Are some of his or her actions or behaviors surprising to you?

Take It or Leave It:

Whether your child is six months, six years, or sixteen years old, hold them close but let them move. Let them figure out their boundaries, what they can do and can't do, while you watch, but don't do everything for them. They're safe with you, so give them the space to explore, grow, and even fall.

Just like with any relationship, having conversations with your children is critical. Keep all lines of communication open. Play a game and ask your child how his or her day is going and then be quiet. Whether it's cards, a video game, or playing catch, let your child talk while you listen. Try to refrain from giving unsolicited advice, but communicate that you're there for your child if he or she needs help. Just like adults, sometimes kids need to vent and get stuff off their chests, but they're not always looking for you to step in. If your children trust that you'll listen and not just tell them what they should or should not do, they'll be more likely to come to you when they need and want your advice and assistance.

I promised myself, and Eric, that I would never stop working on our ever-evolving relationship. It hasn't been easy, but I've come to trust and believe that Eric is more than capable of being in charge of all aspects of his life. But for as long as I live, all he needs to do is say the word, and I will be by his side in a second. Make that a heartbeat. Guaranteed.

Now to work on that other ever-changing relationship—marriage.

Oh No, You Didn't

You Did What?!

Crisis:
Love on the Rocks Till
Chores Do Us Part

Marc is neat and organized. However, in some ways, he still leaves a trail wherever he goes. There's the coffee cup next to the front door where he took the last sip, put the cup down, picked up his keys, and left for the day. There's the remote control he put down at the foot of the bed from watching CNBC while putting on his suit. Somehow his socks never make it into the bathroom clothes bin, resting instead on the floor by the bed. I can tell precisely where Marc has been, and what he was doing, based on the trail of evidence left behind.

Then there's his "Did I ever tell you about the time …" stories. I don't understand how the man can get so excited to tell the same stories over and over again. After being married all these years, it's pretty easy to spot when Marc is all ramped up and launching into another thrilling tale from *Golf's Greatest Hits and Misses*. As soon as he reaches the most exciting part of his high-suspense golf adventure story, Marc takes a quick breath, brushes the tip of his nose with his hand in a fast motion, and with bright eyes and a big smile quickens his pace while taking the listener through an exhilarating eighteen-hole play-by-play. And every time this happens, I nod my head, listen, and smile right back at him as if I've never heard such a thrilling tale in all my life.

Dear Lord, grant me the strength to listen to his doglegged-left-stroke-splice-yard-swing, yadda, yadda, yadda golf stories for the rest of my life. Without your help, I might need to lose my mind!

While we're dishing the dirt on Marc, I also need to tell you that he's a loud chewer. I don't know if the people at adjoining tables in a restaurant can hear him, but I sure as heck can when he's sitting across from me. After tens of thousands of meals together, I'd think he'd be able to quiet that chomper of his.

I know you're thinking, *Jeez, Margarete, you sound very picky! All the stories you've ever told about Marc make it sound like you have a fairy-tale romance. What's going on?*

Well, let me tell you something, a little secret about my husband that I've been holding onto for the thirty years we've been married. It's not easy to admit, so I'm just going to say it: Marc is a … well, he's kind of … um …. Here it goes: Marc is entirely human. There, I've said it. The cat's out of the bag. Despite appearances to the contrary, Marc is not the perfect Prince Charming, and I have a bunch of pet peeves about his behavior. But hey, don't you feel the same about your spouse or partner? C'mon, let it loose and let those complaints fly!

But wait, before you start your list, there's more about Marc I can complain about. I'm on a roll. Don't stop me now. Here's more Cassalina dirty laundry I can air and get off my chest.

Marc doesn't know how to load a dishwasher properly, and his idea of sweeping the floor involves swishing a broom around willy-nilly while he's talking on the phone, probably sharing some ridiculous golf story. Getting him to remember to pick up the dry-cleaning is hit or miss at best. But you can be sure he never forgets his Wednesday night golf game, and if he could only apply a little of that golf swing to the broom, just think how clean our floors would be. Am I just dreaming here, people? I'm sure I'm not the only one who has to deal with such domestic inabilities, don't you agree? Don't you feel the same way about your spouse or partner?

Don't get me wrong; the man is smart. He's very smart when it comes to investments and all things business, but why do all those smarts leave his brain the second he needs to put some glasses in the dishwasher or put a new roll of toilet paper in the bathroom? Do you think he does these things to annoy me or because he doesn't value me? Maybe it's because he doesn't care about what I do or say. Has golf unseated me as the most important thing is his life? You know, I'm starting to think I made a major mistake in kissing this Prince Charming, because he's looking more and more like a toad every day!

Whoa, Margarete! Wait a minute! You are heading in the wrong direction. Apply the brakes immediately! All of this runaway brain chitter-chatter is nothing but fake news! It's time to jump out of that Cinderella carriage, switch brain-wave channels, and get some positive vibes coming through instead!

Phew! Now that I've chilled out a bit and given myself a severe reality check, I can say the stone-cold truth is that Marc does value me, and he cares deeply about what I think and how I'm feeling, even if he forgets the dry-cleaning and puts the glasses on the bottom rack with the Tupperware lids. Even if he can't remember where the laundry basket is, he shows me how important I am by being there in the ways he best knows how: looking over speaking contracts, reading and providing feedback on my stories, articles, and speeches, and making sound investment decisions for the money I earn. When all is said and done, I have to admit I'm lucky to have my husband also be my #1 fan and an active supporter of my work. And it doesn't hurt that he likes to surprise me with wine and flowers for no other reason than to say I love you.

So let me tell you another little secret: in *my* eyes and my heart, Marc *is* my Prince Charming. He's 100 percent human, no doubt about it, but every single day since January 16, 1990, he has told me that he loves me. And I know that's *real news* because I've said the same to him—every single day. After thirty years of sharing a life with him, I don't have any pet peeves about that.

I am not a marriage counselor, but I do know that every marriage has two people in it—two people who will have unique habits and quirks. We are all unique, and we all see the world a bit differently. That's all great if we can decide to accept our differences, appreciate the positives peacefully, and live happily ever after. But it doesn't change the fact that some of those quirks are downright nerve wracking and irritating! Oh! I'm getting all worked up again just thinking about it! C'mon, don't you think the loud chewing is more than a woman should have to bear? No? Well, what about those glasses on the bottom rack of the dishwasher? Who would put plastic lids on the bottom rack?? I mean, really? Or twenty years of never-ending golf stories? Once I start down this path, it's so easy to go around and around in an endless spiral of negativity (Have I told you about the socks on the floor?). When I focus my attention on Marc's qualities that I don't like, it's easy to ignore the parts I cherish and treasure so much. And *that* is a problem I cannot live with.

One of the unfortunate side effects of reaching midlife is that many of my friends, both male and female, have separated from or divorced their spouses. It's sad to see a marriage disintegrating; it's a bit like watching a sandcastle melting into the ocean's waves. Over time, all the pet peeves and irritations build and grow into overwhelming problems that ultimately become "irreconcilable differences." I'm pretty sure these marriages didn't dissolve over differences in chewing food or the stories told at dinner parties, but I firmly believe that even the best of marriages can unravel. And that unraveling begins because two people fail to stop the molehill from growing into a mountain. What starts as an annoyance over household chores, grocery shopping, or doing the laundry grows into routine arguments about work schedules, family commitments, and personal time. Then, before you know it, you're choosing to be surrounded by strangers in a bar instead of going home, or finding ways to avoid one another even when you're in the same house. Once you've reached this point, you've got a mountain wedged into your marriage that can't easily be removed.

My divorced friends say their relationships drifted apart or that they couldn't get along anymore, and many, if not all, left their spouses for someone else. When I would ask if they had tried talking to one another about their marital problems or entering into couple's therapy, the answers I often heard were "My spouse won't talk to me" or "He [or she] won't listen to what I'm trying to say" or "We tried it once. It's not for us. It's just pointless." Honest communication and honest listening, even when it hurts, is critical to keeping a marriage together, but all too often it's the hardest thing to do.

Some friends, before they got divorced, would complain almost incessantly about their spouse's most annoying trait. You know, that one thing that would drive them crazy. Like loud chewing. Like glasses in the bottom of the dishwasher. Like socks on the floor or forgotten dry-cleaning.

Once started, they'd move from the #1 annoying habit to all the other annoying traits. The offending spouse is not exercising anymore, is gaining weight, is not helping around the house, or is not socializing or refusing to go out together. They recall any and all spousal traits that drive them nuts, and then they add even more negative feelings and habits to the list. Once a person reaches a prolonged level of anger and disaffection, no one, including me, is surprised when the separation and divorce come along. Strangely enough, when this happened to longtime friends, I was able to remember when they were younger, in love, and feeling like every little thing they did was magic. Over time they went from being so close they could complete each other's sentences to not being close enough to hold hands at the dinner table. It breaks my heart just thinking about it.

Someone once told me that the trait you love most about a person in the early days of your relationship is the same trait that will drive you nuts later on in life. Hmm. I don't recall ever loving the way Marc chewed.

My point is that we all have habits that are annoying (if Marc ever writes a book, I'm sure he'll tell you mine). If you let the small irritants become huge ones, you're going to very quickly become dissatisfied and unhappy with your partner and your life, and before you know it, you'll be calling 1-800-DIVORCE. What you feed will grow, good or bad. Don't feed the negative. Build up the good stuff.

Divorce is a big thing. It wreaks havoc on your mental, physical, and financial well-being. It creates chaos for both the young and adult-aged children you may have, as well as for your mutual friends and family. I realize that divorce is necessary sometimes, and it can be the best and only course of action when significant differences are truly irreconcilable. Call me old-fashioned, but I still think divorce should be an exception and not a rule. When I hear some of the reasons why marriages fail, I have to scratch my head and wonder. Do they think the next person who comes into their life will be a perfect replacement who will forever read their mind, do everything exactly as they wish, and never have a bad day or gain an extra pound or tell a story over and over again? We're all 100 percent human 100 percent of the time, pet peeves and all. Maybe that second marriage will be the charm, but if you don't accentuate the positive and appreciate the good qualities, then spouse #2 will start looking like spouse #1 pretty darn quick!

Here's My Take

It's easy to say that no one is perfect, but it's much harder to live by those words and accept the imperfect behaviors of those closest to us. Why do we make small, annoying habits bigger than they are? Why do we find fault and then repeatedly obsess on it until it drives us nuts?

Early on in our marriage, Marc and I established the 80/20 rule. The idea behind it is that if you concentrate on the 20 percent that drives you nuts about your spouse, like the chewing, socks, or stories, that 20 percent will seem a whole lot bigger than it truly is, and in no time it will consume your emotions and dictate how you feel. Your aggravation will grow, and pretty soon just looking at your spouse will get you all worked up. You'll be less likely to say "I love you," give them a kiss or a hug, or hold their hand and more likely to stop talking to each other, leave the room, and go to bed at different times. Soon, the emotional bonds that brought you together will start to weaken and unravel.

My pet peeve of Marc not loading the dishwasher properly would fall into that 20 percent. I could choose to get very upset at his inability to learn how to do this task correctly. I could then add the dishwasher irritation to my frustration with his leaving the morning coffee cup by the front door. And then when he arrives home without the dry-cleaning, I can refuse to even look at him because I'm confident he's done all of this to aggravate me, failing to think about me and caring less about what's important to me.

So, instead of getting bent out of shape, I say, "Yup, that's part of the

20 percent," and turn my focus to all the wonderful traits Marc has. And like most of us, he has a ton of them. He makes me coffee each morning and brings it to me in bed. He takes the garbage out every Thursday. I'm always his last call or text as he leaves work. His nickname for me has always been Hottie. He is a super smart guy and a hard worker who has financially provided for our family through heartbreaking, soul-crushing times, and he makes me feel like I'm the best thing that ever walked into his life. The littlest bits that make up this 80 percent are so much more beautiful and inspiring than everything else combined in the 20 percent. I focus on what a bountiful 80 percent I have, and not the stupid dishwasher, when I want to remind myself how much love we honestly have.

As this chapter has disclosed several "secrets," I have one more I want to share with you. In recent years, since our son, Eric, married Kourtney and we became empty nesters, I feel our rule has gone from 80/20 to 90/10. At this stage of my life, I feel like I can love, admire, and adore Marc even more. I gladly choose to see the good qualities, and I remind myself that 10 percent is a perfectly acceptable amount of annoyance as I pick up his coffee mug and place it correctly on the top rack of the dishwasher.

What's Your Take?

What is one thing about your spouse you fell in love with at the beginning of your relationship? What is one thing that drives you nuts about him or her now? Are these two things the same or different? Do you find yourself focusing on the small, annoying traits? How do you feel when you do that? When you focus on the small, annoying characteristics, do you tend to add quickly to that list? Do you feel your emotions grow negative? How often do you focus on the good things your spouse does or the qualities you enjoy? Do you find it hard to rattle off good traits compared to the negative? How does it feel when you bring to mind something you love about your spouse?

Take It or Leave It

The next time you find yourself complaining about your spouse, ask yourself if this habit is part of the 20 percent. If so, counter it with telling yourself two or three things you adore about your spouse. Even with the anger and frustration of the moment, find it. We are all 100 percent human, and we are all trying to love and be loved.

Ask yourself when was the last time you had an emotional heart-to-heart conversation with your spouse about how each other feels. If the thought of doing that makes you laugh out loud, then maybe that's the exact thing you should be doing. If you don't talk and listen to one another, you might find yourself talking (and listening to) a divorce attorney instead.

And while you have that phone in your hand, consider this ...

Obnoxious Ringtones and Coffee

And Suddenly All the Love Songs Were about You

Being Afraid of the Sappy Stuff

I'm at lunch with a girlfriend, and my iPhone begins to softly play an entire verse of my favorite Thompson Square song, "This life would kill me if I didn't have you."

I'd forgotten to put my phone on vibrate, and this song snippet is the sound notification I use to know when I receive a text from my husband, Marc. I hastily explain this as I scramble to dig the phone out of my bag.

"You're kidding, right?" my girlfriend says sarcastically.

I smile. I shrug.

Yeah, it's sappy. It's obnoxiously romantic, totally over the top. And I wouldn't have it any other way.

Now, why can't I find that darn phone?

On August 11, 1989, Marc and I went on our first date, and we've been working on staying sappy ever since. When we were first married, he asked me to name one thing he could do every day that would make me happy. I had to think about it for a bit, but then I told him, "Wake me up with a cup of coffee in the morning." I then asked him the same question, and without hesitation he answered, "A kiss good morning every day, and a kiss before bed every night."

And just like that, a thirty-year tradition began.

Our coffee makers may have changed over the years, but I can always count on Marc to hand me a cup of coffee every morning. It's not the coffee that's made me happy, although it's certainly nice to have; instead, it's the time we spend each morning talking while we're drinking our coffee. Even when life was crazy busy with two children born with cystic fibrosis, we always found the time, even if it was only a few minutes, to enjoy a cup of coffee together.

During our coffee talks, we'd discuss our parenting, our marriage, and our dreams. We'd remind each other of the reasons we were both so crazy busy with family, work, saving money to pay the mortgage and the medical bills, and stress—it was because we had fallen in love back in 1989. We'd remind ourselves that we were a team and that working together to keep that strong was a priority in our lives. Over the years, Marc and I faced many hurdles and obstacles, but by having those fifteen minutes a day together first thing in the morning, it felt like we could make it through anything and everything.

Then, in 2006, we faced our hardest challenge, our biggest fear, and our worst nightmare. We suffered the loss of Jena, our daughter. Cystic fibrosis destroyed her lungs, and there was nothing more medical science could do. On Monday, December 4, 2006, at the age of thirteen, our sweet child moved up to heaven. No amount of morning coffee, talking, or kisses was going to heal our hearts. The loss of a child cuts you to the core, and even if someone is by your side, you alone have to face your emotions.

Marc gave me space to grieve for as long as I needed. I gave him the room to mourn. It wasn't pretty. It was real.

During those seemingly endless dark days, Marc continued to bring me coffee, though many mornings it went cold, untouched. We still sat together, mugs sitting on the bedside table, though often it was in silence or amid a few mumbled words spoken through tears. We had created a family out of love, and the deep pain of even our daily kisses hurt our hearts, though, trembling, still we'd kiss.

So the ringtone song fits. This life very well may have killed us if we hadn't had all those years of just fifteen minutes a day talking and drinking coffee together. Those little things, the sappy things, have been the things we both cling to. They're what pulled us through—together.

Back at the lunch table, I finish texting Marc a reply and switch my iPhone to vibrate. Looking up, I smile to myself to see that my girlfriend is now searching iTunes for a ringtone.

Here's My Take

We all need to acknowledge that little subconscious habits can have a significant impact on a relationship, both positive and negative. Establishing small daily reminders of positive feelings can compound and carry you when you least expect it.

There are still days when I find myself curled up on the floor, feeling very alone and missing Jena desperately. And out of the blue, my iPhone softly sings my favorite Thompson Square song with the lyrics, "This life would kill me if I didn't have you."

Marc's text might be as simple as "I'll be home at 7 p.m.," or "Want to meet for a glass of wine after work?" but hearing the lyrics reminds me that life is a beautiful roller-coaster adventure when you're actively working on the journey—or at least talking about it over a morning cup of coffee.

What's Your Take?

Do you have a special reminder of how important your spouse or significant other is to you? If not, think of the things in your life that remind you of all the good you have together. Is it a certain song? lines from a movie? the scent of perfume or aftershave? Find something you can reach for, read, or hear that will put you in a positive emotional mood while reminding you of what you love so much about your special loved one.

Take It or Leave It

What are you waiting for? Start creating your strong habits today. Set up a ringtone or a text notification that puts your heart in the right place when your spouse reaches out to you, or start a daily ritual that involves your spouse. Ask each other what's the one simple thing that you can do every day to make each other happy. Commit to doing that one thing for thirty days, and by the end of the month, your happiness habit will feel perfectly natural and essential. And just think, when you openly embrace the sappy and romantic, your vibe becomes contagious!

What's not romantic is getting drugged … at a bar.

Officer, I Was Drugged

Crisis:
A Fun Night Out Turns Dangerous

It was August 2004, and Marc and I, along with three other couples, were out celebrating our friend Tara's fortieth birthday. As we finished our dinner, we realized it was only 8:30 p.m., so we decided to go to a nearby restaurant that doubles as a club for an after-dinner drink and a little dancing. What a great idea, we all thought, just like the old days when we were young and carefree.

Upon arriving, a few of us went up to the bar to order drinks. While I waited for my Cosmopolitism and Marc's martini, I had a chance to look around at the bar staff, cocktail waitresses, and club-goers and think about how much time I'd spent at places like this before Marc and I met and settled down with a family. While I was having my happy trip down memory lane, I noticed the uncomfortable expression of the bouncer, standing at the end of the bar. He appeared to be in his forties and was well over six feet tall and two hundred pounds. Not the kind of guy you'd want to get on the wrong side of, but he was looking at me.

With our drinks in hand, the eight of us sat down at a long table and continued our conversations. A cocktail waitress approached our group, and we ordered another round of drinks just as the DJ started playing some

EMBRACING THE BEAUTY IN THE BROKEN

classic disco and pop songs from the 1970s and '80s. When Madonna's "Lucky Star" came on, all of us women decided to get up and dance while the men stayed back at the table. As we headed out onto the dance floor, we noticed a young woman who seemed to be extremely intoxicated. We laughingly commented about how young people never know their limits and said that she'd probably be quite sick in the morning.

While we were dancing, I noticed that the bouncer from the bar was now leaning against the wall by the dance floor. A few minutes later, he made his way over to me, randomly tapped my arm, and walked away. Because I was feeling a bit uncomfortable by this strange behavior, we moved to the other side of the floor, danced to the rest of the song, and then returned to the table where our husbands were. While we had been dancing, the drinks had arrived, and thirstily I took a few sips of my Cosmo, which tasted delicious.

At around 9:30 p.m., the club was steadily getting more crowded, and the crowd coming in was young with everyone on the dance floor looking like they were in their twenties. We all decided it was time to head home and leave the kids to their fun. I was in total agreement because I was starting to feel a little dizzy and slightly nauseous. In the car heading back to Tara's house, I rolled down the window to get some fresh air, but it didn't help much. When we arrived, I stumbled out of the car and made a beeline for her bathroom. I quickly vomited everything I had consumed that evening and was soon so weak that I couldn't raise my head off the toilet seat. Soon after, I collapsed onto the floor, unable to move, but still able to hear the sounds and voices around me. Slipping in and out of consciousness, I heard Marc call 9-1-1.

Marc explained to the 9-11 operator that I had heart issues and that he knew there was something seriously wrong with me. The EMS arrived, and I could hear them ask where we had been, what I had eaten and drunk, and when I'd started feeling ill. One of the responders placed his fingers in the palm of my hand and directed me to squeeze. I heard his words but couldn't move my hand. I couldn't move anything. I was completely paralyzed. Then I heard him say the words, "It looks like she was roofied."

The next thing I knew, I was in the hospital's ER, hooked up to fluids and having dry heaves. The nurse on duty told Marc that it appeared I had been given the date rape drug Rohypnol, commonly known as a roofie. Marc was shocked and told the nurse we had been together all evening and that the drinks we had ordered had been in clear view the entire time. She said we would need to wait for the toxicology report to confirm if it was Rohypnol, but she said that she had seen my symptoms too many times before.

Around 4:00 a.m. I finally began to feel better. The doctor on call came through with discharge papers. Marc took the discharge sheet and read the diagnosis. "Intoxicated?" he questioned the doctor as he read the diagnosis. "What about the toxicology report? Did they find any drugs in her system?" The doctor said there hadn't been sufficient evidence to support a toxicology screen and that I simply needed to sleep and drink a lot of water.

"We could run a test now, but chances are if she were allegedly drugged, the levels would be so low that it wouldn't show on a regular toxicology report," he replied. Stunned at this unbelievable oversight, but happy I was feeling better, we left the hospital. I spent the rest of the day in bed with a horrible headache.

While I was sleeping, Marc called a friend who was a local police officer to see if he knew anything about the nightclub we had gone to. Upon hearing the story, he told Marc that the place had been under investigation for quite some time, but it was difficult to apprehend the criminal or criminals who were dosing drinks with Rohypnol without an eyewitness who had seen the act. Off the record, he told Marc that certain employees were under suspicion. When Marc expressed his frustration that the ER doctor hadn't run the toxicology screen, his friend explained that unfortunately it was fairly common for some doctors not to run the test. If they ran the test and it came back positive for Rohypnol, there would be a tremendous amount of paperwork plus the likelihood of having to appear in court. Because of that, most doctors would only administer the full drug panel screening if the patient indicated they had been raped. He told Marc that the two young women were found that morning within five hundred feet of the nightclub in just their underwear with visible signs of having been raped, but with no recollection of what happened. They had been roofied.

When Marc relayed this information to me, I was shocked. I had been "the lucky one" who was roofied but hadn't been raped and left on the side of a street for someone to find. That knowledge chilled me to the core. We had done everything right. We had gone out with good friends whom we had known for years, we hadn't had much to drink, and our drinks were always in view. We hadn't stayed out late, but still, at thirty-six years old, I had to worry about someone putting narcotics into my drink. To this day, I still shudder when I think back to that night and those two young women who were not lucky. I pray for them always. I can only imagine what that night did to them. I can only imagine how their lives were forever changed by a seemingly simple night of going out to a club with friends and dancing.

In time, it was exposed that the bartender and the bouncer, along with other employees, worked together to select and drug unsuspecting female victims. When the young women would stumble toward the bathroom because they weren't feeling well, the men took turns "helping" them into a back corridor next to the bathrooms, where they would then rape them. When they were done, they would "escort" the young woman back to her friends, saying their drunk friend had blacked out near the bathroom and that they should take her home right away. But other young women weren't so lucky, and like those who had been drugged the same night I had been, they were merely left outside, unconscious and alone. As only a few sips of my drugged Cosmo rendered me paralyzed and in the ER, I can imagine what would have happened had we stayed to finish that second round of drinks. What would have happened to me if I had finished it? I shudder to think of the possibilities.

❀☙

Here's My Take

I tell this story so that people of all ages can be educated to the dangers of drugged drinks. I was an older married woman out with her husband and friends, and someone slipped drugs into my drink. It impacted my psyche for months. Had I done something wrong? Had I worn something inappropriate? That night haunted me with so many what-ifs. It took a long time for me to feel safe anywhere. I was scared to go anywhere, eat anything, and drink anything, which was not only extremely scary but also eye-opening. Shortly after the incident, I was telling my story to a friend's college-aged kids, and they seemed to be well aware of the dangers. Almost all of these young females said that if they went to a club or party where roofies might be in play, they'd order beer in bottles or cans and keep their thumb over the opening of the bottle themselves. What?! I was mystified and horrified. Instead of demanding change and calling out the predators, they preferred to accept the danger and change their drinking habits. But what about the women who go to a club or party who don't know? What happens to them? That has made me more determined to share my story to shine a light on these disgusting and vile crimes. I know it was not my fault and I had done nothing wrong, but it took me some time to come to that conclusion. All victims are violated. That night took away the certainty of my safety.

What's Your Take?

Has there ever been a time when you were "lucky" to have walked away from a dangerous situation? Or perhaps you were the unsuspecting victim of a violent sexual crime. This is a very sensitive and frightening subject, even if the incident occurred decades ago. Fortunately we're living in a time when more and more women and men who have been assaulted, abused, or harassed are speaking out. Know that you are not alone and that by telling your story and reaching out to others who have undergone similar suffering, you are helping yourself to heal and release the shame and pain you may still have.

Take It or Leave It

There is no doubt that this is an extremely fear-inducing topic. One of the best ways to alleviate that fear is to shine a light into the dark and take the best possible actions so it will not happen again.

It doesn't matter how young or old you are. It doesn't matter if you're "hot" or "not." If you're out at a club or a bar, never leave your drink unattended. Keep an eye on your drink and the drinks of anyone who is with you. If you're going to the restroom or stepping outside to make a call, have a friend keep an eye on your drink for you. And if you do leave your drink unattended for any reason, order a new one. It only takes a second for someone to slip something into a drink without your knowledge. Watch the bartender pour your drink, or open it yourself. Never accept a drink from the hand from a stranger. If someone offers to buy you a drink and you want to accept, walk with them up to the bar and watch it being made and served directly to you.

If you're at a bar, club, or party and begin to feel drunk or sick, seek help and stop drinking immediately to avoid a potentially dangerous situation. Get a friend or someone else who knows you to stay nearby, and let them know if you're feeling dizziness, tingling, mental fogginess, muscle weakness, etc., right away. Do not attempt to go outside or to the restroom alone.

And always be aware of your surroundings. Trust your instincts. If someone is creeping you out, let a friend know, and consider moving to a different location or, better yet, leaving. I remember how that bouncer came up to me and touched my arm and how unsettling it was. I didn't know it at the time, but he was already stalking his next victim, and it was me. I'm so very thankful I managed to get away.

If you are ever the victim of sexual assault or violence, report it to authorities immediately. The National Sexual Assault Hotline operated by RAINN (the Rape, Abuse, and Incest National Network) is a twenty-four-hour crisis hotline staffed by trained professionals who can offer support and guidance.[1]

Educate yourself, stay safe, and never take a snow globe on a plane.

---

[1] Much of the information I provide on what to do when out and drinking alcohol was adapted from https://www.alcohol.org/women/a-night-out-drinking/.

Overpacked

Your Emotional Baggage Exceeds
Our Carry-On Limits

Crisis:
When Your Emotional Baggage
Becomes Too Heavy to Lift

As I place my worn suitcase on the scale at the ticket counter, I'm greeted by a very friendly airline official.

"How many bags are you checking in today?" he asks in a chipper tone.

Looking at the one bag I had placed on the scale, I smirk, point, and say, "One?"

He continues, "Did you pack this bag yourself?"

I give a sarcastic laugh. "Yes, I did. The maid had the day off."

I mean, really, who else would pack my bags? Was this guy trying to be funny? Did he honestly think I was incapable of packing my bag?

His formerly buoyant demeanor disappears, and in rapid fire he rattles off a series of questions without taking a breath:

Did you pack any electronic lighters, e-lighters, or e-cigarettes?

"Did you pack any fireworks, firearms, or flares in your suitcase?

"Do you have any lithium ion and lithium metal batteries, or a laptop?

"Have you packed anywhere on you or in your suitcase a Samsung Galaxy Note 7 cellular phone, a hover board including series T1, T3, and T8, a mini Segway with lithium batteries, or any alcohol over 140 proof?

"Are you traveling with any poisons or radioactive materials such as uranium, thorium, and radon?

"How about a snow globe bigger than a tennis ball?"

Finally, he stops with the questions and takes a breath.

I stare at him like he's suddenly sprouted a third eye in the middle of his forehead. Could he have said that any faster? Was he a professional auctioneer moonlighting as a check-in agent at the airport? Jeez, Buddy, I'm already stressed out because I have a ton of work I need to do on this flight, and this interrogation isn't making it any better. And by the way, what the heck is this thing about a snow globe? Since when did *that* become a contraband item?

I look directly into his eyes and slowly answer as if I were speaking to a small child: "Um, no." I can feel the frustration rising in my chest and throat.

"Oh, and never mind about the snow globe. That question is mainly for carry-on bags. If you do have a snow globe in your purse, you can check it here with me." He offers me a half smile but still sounds annoyed.

Returning his tone and fake smile, I answer, "No. No snow globes in any of my bags today."

"Fine," he continues. "Has anyone asked you to transport anything for them either in your bags or on your physical body?"

Thoughts speed through my mind. Seriously? Do you think I'm a terrorist? Do you think I'm a drug mule? I'm a middle-aged suburban woman from upstate New York who wants to get checked in so I can make my way to my flight and sit down for a few minutes before I start tackling my to-do list. I don't know any known enemies of the state, and I don't even know anyone who does illegal drugs. Who the heck would ask me to carry anything for them? I'm not stupid, you know. I know what you're trying to do here. I'm not going to fall for this nonsense. You're not going to trap me into getting pulled from the line so I can wait in a room while a TSA officer unpacks and inspects my suitcase. I am so not in the mood for this!

And then all of a sudden the danger sign pops into my head. *Pull yourself together, Margarete,* I tell myself. *You're speeding so fast that you're close to spinning out of control. It's time to slow this train of thought down before I do or say something I regret. I don't need to be behaving this way. My manner and attitude isn't helping anyone, least of all myself.*

I shake my head slowly, take a breath, and reply calmly and with a real smile, "No, sir. No one asked me to carry anything for them."

And then the questions come to an end. My suitcase is pushed off down the conveyor, and boarding pass in hand, I make my way toward the next security checkpoint. I promise myself I'll do a better job of staying calm when I have to put my laptop, shoes, and coat into separate bins.

As I walk through the airport, I think about this encounter and the variations of it that have occurred throughout my lifetime, a seemingly innocent question that triggers a negative emotional response because it touches a nerve connected to some deeper issue I haven't resolved. In this case, I knew I was on edge. I was on my way to present at a large national conference, and I was scared. I was afraid I would fail. I was worried I would make significant mistakes. I was regretting the day I'd excitedly agreed to do this. I had all that emotional baggage in addition to my suitcase, and the ticket agent had no idea I was carrying it around. All he got to see was my stressed-out, snarky, sarcastic self. Lucky him. Or, should I say, unlucky him.

To resolve those knee-jerk negative responses, I need to unpack and lighten my emotional baggage. Those old fears and beliefs weigh me down and stress me out and make my life and the lives of those around me less enjoyable and more miserable.

I decide to ditch that unclaimed, no longer needed baggage right there on the concrete tarmac. I want to go to this conference and tell my story to that roomful of people. I want to fly full speed ahead and leave those old insecurities far, far behind.

I tell myself that the next time someone asks me if I've packed my own bags, I will happily, confidently, and most self-assuredly say, "Yes! It was all me!"

Here's My Take

Baggage is an excellent metaphor for your unresolved emotional and psychological beliefs that are triggered when you're in a particular situation.

What has always amazed me is how two people can have the same background, yet one of those people can be downright miserable, blaming everything and everyone for their misery, and the other person can truly enjoy wherever they are, acknowledging their past as part of their journey and looking forward to today and tomorrow. The first person is buried under their baggage, and the second is traveling light, enjoying their fabulous adventure, and embracing the wonderful, beautiful, and secure person they know they are.

I've worked on unpacking so much unwanted baggage that I've lost count how many suitcases full of issues I've left behind. That unpacking didn't happen overnight, and it took years of sorting out where those beliefs came from and deciding if they benefited me or not. The beliefs and behaviors that don't help me are gone. The ones that support and nourish me, I value immensely.

The beliefs I am willing and able to carry are these:

- I am emotionally strong, capable, and smart.
- I am trustworthy, and I choose to trust the world and the people around me.
- I believe I owe it to God and to the world to be all I can be.
- I know my worth, and I decide my value. I don't have to prove that to anyone.

What's Your Take?

What uncalled-for and unfriendly thoughts go through your head? Have you ever asked who put those thoughts there? Who packed your belief system? Think about any bottled-up anger and unresolved feelings that travel with you everywhere you go. How long have those feelings been getting a free ride with you? Can you remember when these behaviors or reactions began?

Do any of the following thoughts, feelings, or beliefs ever cross your mind?

- I don't trust people. They will only let me down and take advantage of me.
- I'm not good enough. I can't do anything right. Why even try?
- I need someone to take care of me. I can't even trust my own decisions.
- Good things happen to other people, not me.
- No one listens to me, and no one cares what I think or how I feel.
- I'm not smart enough.
- I don't have value.
- I don't expect much from people because they only let me down.
- I build a wall for protection because if others knew the real me, they wouldn't like it. They might leave.
- I'm defensive because you're just going to hurt me anyway. I won't let you get close to me.

Are you carrying a suitcase full of defensive attitudes, secret fears, or unprocessed anger? Is your luggage loaded with shame, embarrassment, and feelings of abandonment?

Maybe an overbearing father instilled fear and shame if you didn't measure up to a certain standard. Maybe an overprotective mother did everything for you, and you feel inadequate to handle the world. Perhaps you have been abandoned by people you depended on. Perhaps you're distrustful of people after having been hurt by an unfaithful lover or spouse. Are you still fighting with those people in your head while the innocent, unsuspecting person in front of you gets hit with the brunt of your overpacked emotional baggage?

Take It or Leave It

Think about the last time you blurted out hateful words or behaved in a rash manner because of your feelings of heated anger. How did you feel immediately afterward? Did your emotional response meet the situation at hand, or were you over the top? Were you feeling regret or the need to apologize? Ask yourself why that thought, that emotion, or that action was even there was in the first place. Decide if it's a thought or a feeling that benefits you. When you address that, you'll be amazed at how much lighter your baggage will become.

If you can read the signs, that is.

Obstacles Are Opportunities

Crisis:
Backward and Upside Down

How I see math word problems:

Q. If you have $13 and I lose 71 hexagons, how many miles will you go before the velocity of pizza is Jupiter?

A. Roses, because 9.8 degrees is marbles.

In 1975 I was diagnosed with dyslexia. I was in the second grade, and my reading skills had hit a wall. I confused my E's and my 3's, and it was a challenge figuring out the difference between b, d, p, and q. My teacher sent me to the nurse's office for a screening, and that afternoon I was given a note addressed to my parents explaining I had a learning disorder called dyslexia. I wondered, was it contagious?

I don't know how my parents responded to the note or if they ever spoke to the nurse or my classroom teacher. But I do know that they never talked to me about the diagnosis or what it meant. Even though other kids in school sometimes left the room for extra help, I never did. Instead, I struggled to figure out the words on a page, and I struggled to write my own words down. My penmanship was far from beautiful. It always took me longer to read and comprehend a paragraph or page compared to my classmates, and remembering multistep directions was difficult if they weren't written down. When I compared myself to other kids at school, I often felt inadequate and self-conscious.

My saving grace was that I knew I wasn't dumb, and I loved going to school. I enjoyed learning new things and listening to my teachers. Even though I had to move my lips during silent reading time, I did it because it helped me to understand the words. I didn't stop even if some kids teased me. In the privacy of my room at home, I'd read everything out loud. Then, after reading aloud, I'd either highlight or write down what I felt the chapter or essay was about. I was passionate about taking notes. When seventh grade began, I received my first hand-me-down typewriter, and it helped me immensely. I'd take notes in class, then go home and transcribe them using the typewriter so they were easier to read. All these typewritten notes went into my Trapper Keeper binder for safekeeping. When it was time for a quiz or test, I'd reread the notes and highlight the critical parts. I worked hard, probably twice as hard as most of my friends, but I wanted to get good grades. I wanted to be liked by my teachers, and I didn't want anyone to know how embarrassed I felt because of my struggles.

As a mother, I have found that these study skills enabled me to learn all about cystic fibrosis and what it meant for Eric and then Jena. At every doctor's appointment, I'd take notes about what was said and then transcribe them into their respective color-coded three-inch binder. Then I'd reread and highlight the essential parts to make sure I understood everything I needed to be aware of and the precise directions for administering their medications. Learning became a matter of life or death, and I was committed to doing whatever needed to be done to understand all the science and medical terminology and commit it to memory.

If life gives you melons, *you may be dyslexic.* (I still read that quote as mentioning lemons and not melons.)

The first few years of marriage and motherhood were such a whirlwind that I rarely had time to think back and remember my childhood, but in 1996 an incident occurred that brought it all flooding back. Eric was five years old at the time and was having a hard time pronouncing certain words. He was also writing many numbers and letters backward. His kindergarten teacher suggested testing for learning disabilities, so I made an appointment for an educational evaluation at the regional resource center. While we were in the waiting room, my eyes were drawn to a poster on the wall that, at first glance, appeared to say, "If you can read this, you're dyslexic." I thought to myself, *Gee, that's a pretty stupid message,* until I looked at it again, up close. My second inspection revealed it was a poster that mixed up word order and letters with pictures. To someone who wasn't dyslexic, the message would have been a jumble, but to my brain, which sees patterns but sometimes transposes the order, it made sense. That poster spoke to the way my brain functions.

I was stunned. I sat there dumbfounded, recalling a lifetime of my struggles in school. I don't know how long I stood there in amazement, remembering how hard it was for me to take tests, to read, to think, and to comprehend. I knew I had been diagnosed and felt sad for the seven-year-old me who had been left on my own to figure things out.

At the resource center, I grabbed every pamphlet about dyslexia I could find, and then before going home, we stopped at the bookstore so I could get a deeper understanding of what it all meant. When Eric's evaluation results were released, we discovered that, thankfully, he was not dyslexic. In fact, he was ahead of his age group in cognition, but he was behind his age group in articulation, and he needed glasses. I was relieved that Eric would be spared the hardships I had encountered, but reading over the pamphlets and books helped me to unravel my life of learning challenges.

Even as an adult, I find that phone numbers and directions are my biggest problem. I need the person to speak slowly and clearly so I can write the information down, then I repeat it back to make sure I didn't get it wrong. It may take me a bit longer to read a book, compute a word problem, or take notes verbatim, but I get there. These are challenges, but I have learned to compensate, and with so many advancements in technology, from spell check to Siri, I now have more strategies and solutions at my fingertips than ever before.

But I don't want you to think dyslexia is nothing but bad news. There are benefits to having a mind that's different. I am an extremely thorough person. I have a great memory and can easily spot patterns and concepts. And I'm the undefeated Boggle champion in our family. While everyone else is struggling to find words, all those mixed-up letters make perfect sense to me!

Dyslexia is a part of me. I can't fix it or cure it. I could let it frustrate and limit me, but instead I try to use it as an opportunity to view things differently, to use unique solutions to solve problems, and to see the world from a different angle than most people do. Based on my reading and research on the subject, I discovered that between 5 percent and 10 percent of the population has dyslexia. Those with dyslexia are often people who are "picture thinkers" and highly creative. Perhaps it's not so surprising that I turned out to be a writer. Because of how my brain is wired, I've spent all of my life preparing for this path.

Here's My Take

In hindsight, I'm glad my parents responded as they did when the school nurse sent that note home in 1975. Their decision kept me where I was, and while that meant school was more challenging, it forced me to come up with solutions, taught me how to problem solve, and gave me perspective on the limitations we all have. While I had to work hard, I did do well. If I had viewed my dyslexia as something that was "wrong" with me, I think I would have subconsciously limited myself. Had I received the extra help and individual tutoring that other students were given, it may have been easier to take tests and do homework, but I wouldn't have learned how to assimilate into the world of my peers, and I may not have tried as hard as I did in math and reading comprehension.

Even when I was a slow reader who moved her lips with every word, reading was enjoyable. I loved being transported to different places and times in history and becoming fully immersed in the lives of the characters. Now, thanks to podcasts and services like Audible, I fly through more books and learn more about the subjects that interest me than ever before. Through the obstacle of dyslexia, I found strengths I didn't realize I had. Hardships, challenges, and pain points are in your life for a reason—so you can learn from them and grow in body, mind, and spirit. Don't lose that critical lesson. If you need to, it's okay to write it down, type it out, and reread it with a highlighter in hand.

What's Your Take?

Do you, or did you, have any learning or physical obstacles you have to overcome? What opportunities or strengths were revealed as a result? Do you feel that the obstacle you were presented with was a blessing in disguise or a curse?

Take It or Leave It

If you have any questions about dyslexia, you can go to www.Dyslexia. com and see if you have any of the thirty-seven common traits. Remember, obstacles are just opportunities in disguise. Keep working on your strategies and solutions, and the rewards will be 100 percent yours.

It always better to own the 100 percent that makes you, especially your weaknesses, because they build your strengths.

Owning It

Crisis:
Not Seeing Your Strengths

Owning your story is the bravest thing you can ever do.
—Brené Brown

"Promise me you'll always remember: You're braver than you believe and stronger than you seem, and smarter than you think."
—Christopher Robin to Pooh (A. A. Milne)

Never in my wildest dreams would I have imagined the path this life has taken me down. Back in the early days of motherhood and family life, when every day was full of challenges and struggles, if anyone had prophesied that I would become an award-winning author of two books, a motivational speaker, a freelance writer, and a national advocate for the Cystic Fibrosis Foundation, I would have said they were nuts. Back in the days when I was fearfully navigating my way through health issues and praying for the stamina to run a quarter mile without stopping, if anyone had told me that I'd take up extreme hiking and trek across the Grand Canyon in 102° heat for twenty-seven miles in one day, I would have said they were nuts. And if anyone had told me on January 12, 1991, that I would stay married to my handsome best friend for twenty-eight years (and counting) and that we'd successfully weather storms together, in sickness and in health, I would have said it was a long shot at best.

When I was a kid, a teenager, and a young adult, I didn't see myself as someone with many possibilities. I never saw my inner strength or what I was capable of. But someone knew. Call it God, the universe, or my soul, but something deep inside kept leading me, one step at a time, to do more, to be more. When I started taking those steps, I had no idea what it would lead to, but along the journey I learned. I've learned so much.

What Would the Expert Do?

One of the first steps I took was to seek advice from people who knew what they were doing and why they were doing it. When I paid attention to how people who were experts in their respective fields made decisions and took action, I no longer felt like I was reinventing the wheel when it came to solving my problems. That saved me hours of frustration and made me realize that applying the "What would [fill in the name of the person you want to emulate] do?" rule helped by providing a decision-making framework.

For example, when Eric was young and I decided I wanted to raise funds for the Cystic Fibrosis Foundation, I listened to Doris. I paid attention to what she did, how she did it, and what she said. She was an expert, and by following her advice and guidance, I quickly learned what I needed to do. And then I did it, over and over and over again, until I, too, started to become an expert.

I'm fortunate that I've always had a love for learning and that it's something I have carried with me since I was a child. Life presents us with lots of decisions to make, and the more information we have and the more experiences we have, the better equipped we are to deal with everything from the simplistic and comfortable to the excruciatingly hard choices.

But I'll admit that I can get overwhelmed when I'm presented with too many choices. I have been known to walk into a mall and immediately turn around and walk out because the sheer volume of merchandise is too overwhelming for me to deal with. My girlfriends joke about my "genetic aversion" to shopping, and it's generally true unless I'm looking for new shoes. There's no aversion to a beautiful pair of heels.

Considering my general dislike for shopping malls, department stores, and any store that features dozens of choices for any given item, you can only imagine how I felt when Marc and I decided to undertake a massive renovation of our house. In the nearly three decades we had lived there, spending our money on family well-being and experiences we could share was always our number one priority, and general upkeep and "house stuff" was much farther down the list. When Eric got married and moved out two years ago, we looked around our home and realized it needed some serious TLC. We still had the hand-me-down furniture we had received as a wedding present, and the color mauve, a favorite back in the 1990s, was everywhere! The bathrooms, the living room, the bedroom, were all covered in pink stripes or pink flowers or pink carpet. I jokingly said we were living in a Fountain of Youth house because when you entered it, you felt like you had been transported back to the 1990s. I'm pretty sure Marc's hair gel and my Aqua Net hairspray are buried somewhere in a faux mauve marble bathroom drawer.

In addition to remodeling the house, we also decided to get all new furniture, new appliances, and new bed and bath linens. This decision presented me with a new dilemma. We now had so many more decisions to make. We decided to start small, so we went out on a Saturday afternoon to buy some new towels. Seems easy enough, right? We walked into a department store, and I headed over to the towel section while Marc went to check out kitchen appliances. I knew we wanted towels that were white or gray, but once I saw all the options, I froze. I had no idea that white can also be eggshell, cream, linen, vanilla, ivory, off-white, snow white, winter white ... And don't even get me started on how many shades of gray there are! Then I had to figure out if I wanted organic cotton, hyrdocotton, or jacquard towels. Did I want quick-drying, heathered, or sculpted towels? Did I want classic or bamboo? With my head feeling like it was going to explode, I dashed out of the towel aisle quicker than you can say "But wait, there's more!"

Eager to leave the store, I promptly made my way over to the kitchen section, where Marc was looking at a shelf full of blenders. If picking out towels overwhelmed me, how on earth was I going to make decisions about the critical and more expensive items like beds, couches, and dining room furniture? As I tried to grab his arm to drag him out to the car, a saleswoman walked over and cheerfully asked, "I see you've been looking at the Vitamix. Do you have any questions about it?" Abruptly, I answered with a "No, we were just leaving." only to have Marc follow my words with "Actually, I do have some questions," followed by that damn smile of his. Ugh.

My escape thwarted, I tried to focus on the conversation as the saleswoman explained the difference between the six blenders on display. At some point, the discussion evolved into how we were doing a complete home renovation and how we were feeling challenged by all the interior design choices.

In retrospect, we were very fortunate to have the saleswoman arrive when she did, because had we left the store, we would never have learned about the home design service they offered through the store and its various affiliated partners. We were in the right place at the right time, and when Marc raised the question about needing help, we received more than we expected. My eyes lit up with tears, and I said, "You can help us with this *whole* process?"

The saleswoman grinned and said, "Yup!" I felt like a miracle had just happened.

Three months later, our entire house was decorated from potholders to bedroom furniture, thanks in large part to the talents of the store's interior designers. (Shout out to Alison and Jayne!) And in case you're wondering, our towels are eco-friendly, hydrocotton, gray-mist, fast-drying Turkish cotton, and Marc is quite pleased with his Vitamix A3500, which he uses to make breakfast smoothies—healthy, delicious, and no loud chewing. I am a delighted and thankful woman. When Marc and I are out of our league, struggling to make choices in an area where we aren't experts, we gladly take a helping hand. Willingly and gratefully.

Focus on your strengths, not your weakness

An integral part of our renovation was the creation of a penny floor in our foyer as a way to honor the memory and spirit of our daughter, Jena.

We call found pennies "Jena pennies," and we consider them a symbol of love and of Jena's love from above. Here's a passage from *Beyond Breathing* that explains our floor's meaning:

> In the weeks and months after the funeral, I was inundated with calls from friends and family who just had to tell me a story about how they found this certain penny in the strangest place, and they just knew it was from Jena. One person had found it in the center of her bed after she had just finished making it; the other had found one on the counter where she was sure it had not been a minute earlier.
>
> Everyone seemed to know the story about the penny we found at the funeral home.
>
> After the burial, five-hundred-plus people had gone back for fellowship at Saint Mary's Hall. I barely remember the day, only that I was holding a picture of Eric and Jena in my hand. It was the very same picture I had taped to her bed in Pittsburgh so all the doctors and nurses could see how beautiful she was and what a great smile she had and that she was so much more than what they saw all hooked up to tubes and machines. This picture was like a security blanket for me, and I knew that. I told myself I would throw it away at the end of the day. I was trying so hard to work at moving forward.
>
> At the cemetery, it was windy, and the picture almost fell into the newly dug hole, the hole where Jena's wrapper would be placed. I was so thankful when I grabbed it quickly before it fell in. I held it tighter the rest of the day until we got to the hall. People were all around us, wanting to console us, but somehow it was more like we were consoling them. They had lost her too, and they were in so much pain. I had placed the picture on top of a pile of sympathy cards next to the plate of food that someone had brought me so I could hug and console those who needed it. My childhood friend Debbie had

given me a small angel that I was also holding on to, and I placed the angel on top of the picture so I wouldn't lose it.

I don't know how much time had passed, but people were leaving, and I was still standing in the same place, holding people as they came to comfort me. I looked down, and the plate of food I had never touched was now gone, and the table had been cleared. The sympathy cards were there and so was the angel, but the picture of Eric and Jena was gone.

I panicked. I looked under the table, on the floor, and on each chair and there was no picture to be found. Within seconds I had half a dozen people also looking for the picture.

"I was the one who was supposed to throw it out!" I cried.

"We'll find it," Tara said, not really sure she could keep that promise.

People were now looking through the garbage for the picture of Eric and Jena. I had alarmed just about everybody left in the hall. There I was, a mother who just buried her child, and all I wanted was to have this picture back. I knew it was just a picture, but I was the one who was to decide when I was ready to throw it out. It should have been my choice. I needed to control at least something. I was going to let the picture go, damn it; at least let me control a picture. I knew I was out of control, and I knew it wasn't pretty. Just then Tara's son Dean came over to us.

"Mom," he said. "You have to see this."

She looked over at him as if to say, *Not now.*

But Dean grabbed her arm and brought her over to what seemed at first glance to be a spill of wine or soda on the floor. She looked down at the mess on the floor and looked up at me, her eyes wide. I walked a few steps closer and couldn't believe my eyes. There on the floor, under a table, was a penny, and it was in the center of a perfect heart-shaped spill of wine.

You could not have drawn a more perfect heart if you tried. Jena and I used to tell each other, "Heart to heart, that's what we are," and there on the floor was my answer. I knew Jena left that message for me that day, to remind me—because I had obviously forgotten—that she and I are "heart to heart" and that no thrown-out picture could prevent us from staying that way. I no longer needed my security blanket picture; my penny from heaven told me we would forever be heart to heart.

That would be the perfect story of pennies from heaven, but Marc's story is even better.

It was late one Thursday evening in May, and my cell phone rang.

"You won't believe this one," Marc blurted out.

"Try me," I dared him.

"I just picked up the RV in Jersey, and I was thinking of Jena and missing her. I thought I felt my cell phone vibrate, so I picked it up and saw that no one had called. You know how I have that picture of her on my phone?" He paused for me to answer.

"Yes ... yes ... I know. And ..." I coaxed him along.

"Well, I look at her picture, blow her a kiss, and tell her I miss her. I close the phone and put it back on my hip, and I keep driving along. I put on old country music just like she and I used to sing to, and I swear I felt like she was with me. I say out loud, 'Jena J in the RV,' and just then I hear a loud *ping* on the dashboard. It startles me, and I almost drive off the road. I look down, and smack in front of me is a shiny new penny—heads up! Can you believe it?"

My mouth was open as he was telling me this. I didn't even get a second to respond before he added, "No sooner do I say, 'Hey there, Jena J,' than another one falls out of nowhere!"

"Wow!" was the only thing I got in.

"Well, I just had to tell you. I'll be home in about an hour."

I love that story, but it doesn't end there. A few weeks went by, and Marc needed to go pick up the RV from people who had rented it at West Point for a graduation. It was only about a forty-five-minute drive south, and Marc and I hadn't spent much time together lately, so I agreed to go. I hated riding in the RV. It hurt too much, knowing the only reason we'd gotten it was Jena. We were trying to sell it, but something that big doesn't sell overnight, so in the meantime we were still renting it out.

It was a beautiful spring afternoon, and we got to West Point in no time. Marc checked around the RV to make sure everything was in order before we left. I thought of his story about the pennies, and I searched the compartments above the dashboard to see if I could see anything. Nope, nothing; I just saw a matchbook and a plastic straw. I put my hand in and felt around, just in case I'd missed something. Nope. I pulled down the visor and checked there too. Nope, no change to be found anywhere. Okay, my own inspection was complete, and off we went. We talked about Jena and the RV. Marc agreed it was time to sell it, and he was sad about all the memories we wouldn't be making in it anymore. Just as he was talking, *Ping!*—out fell a penny, landing directly in front of him on the dashboard, heads up. We looked at each other and smiled.

"You're right, Jena," he said, looking out into the sky and continuing to talk to her. "We'll still make memories wherever we go. I love you, too. Jena J in the RV again!"

I grab the penny and look at the year. It's 1967, the year Marc was born. I know that penny was for him, and I know it came from Jena.

When we got home, I ran upstairs and put the penny in my special rose box, where I keep all my pennies from heaven. It's the best investment plan for the past I can think of.

Yes, I still have that 1967 penny, and yes, that will be added to the floor.

Our contractor, who performed admirably throughout all stages of the renovation, relinquished his responsibility when it came to the penny floor. He'd never done one before and didn't want to start with us. Looking at the unfinished foyer, I wondered how we would do this. How many pennies would we need? To further complicate the calculations, our foyer isn't square. It has steps, a small hallway, and a living room entryway to consider, and the walls are slightly off in dimension. Numbers are my weakness, but calculations are Marc's strength, so I let him figure the square footage of the multidirectional foyer, the size of a penny, and how many would be needed to fill in the floor. While he was measuring and calculating, I sketched out a design that would look good in the space, and when we had finished, he showed me, in his precise mathematical way, what we needed to achieve our goal. The penny floor would become a reality and a highlight of our newly renovated home.

Over my lifetime I've learned to identify and focus on the things I am good at instead of wishing I could turn my weaknesses into strengths. Marc is so gifted when it comes to anything involving numbers that even with all the computation gadgets in the world, I still wouldn't catch up to him. I, on the other hand, am a very creative person. I'm also a natural organizer, and I use those two traits to solve problems big and small. These are the qualities and strengths that I love about myself and that my friends and family also value. When I think about being the best person I can be, I don't think about improving my math abilities; I think about how I can use my creative thinking and organizational skills to do good in the world.

To quote Jerry Garcia and the Grateful Dead, "What a long, strange trip it's been." And I'm so glad I dared to embrace the life I was destined to have, step by step.

Here's My Take

I recently went to Ulta Beauty, a humongous overwhelming store full of makeup and hair products. I was looking for a particular brand of foundation and some shampoo. Rather than becoming stressed out by all the choices and trying to locate what I was looking for, I quickly found a sales associate. She took one look at my hair and facial complexion and located exactly what I wanted and needed. In no time, I was out the door, and my blood pressure hadn't risen one bit. Could I have figured out on my own where the items were located? Sure. But I know if I ask someone who is an expert for help, the process will be easier and I'll get what I need. There's nothing to be ashamed of when you need directions and ask for help.

When you own your strengths and your weaknesses, you can play up the former and learn to work around the latter. Use that knowledge as a starting point to expand your thoughts and actions and to know what works best for you.

I might not have studied science beyond high school, but I learned a thing or two from eleventh-grade physics class that I use every single day. Take the law of inertia for example: an object at rest stays at rest, and an object in motion remains in motion with the same speed and the same direction unless acted upon by an unbalanced force.

Don't let your mind become lazy, and don't let unbalanced forces distract you from your forward motion. Never forget that you are designed to be strong and resilient. Underneath the fears and insecurities, we are all superheroes. We need to let those superpowers shine.

What's Your Take?

Does making choices overwhelm you? Do you get frustrated to the point of disgust with processes you can't figure out? Do you put yourself down when you struggle with things that come quickly to others? Sometimes that can be a sign that you need to make improvements in your life, but other times, it's better to acknowledge that each person has special gifts and that we're all unique. What are your strengths and the qualities you're most proud of?

Take It or Leave It

Make a list of all your strengths in one column and your perceived weaknesses in the other. Ask yourself if your weaknesses are something you'd like to change, work on, or add to your strengths. Or are they better left where they are? Focus on your strengths, and as they grow, you can better manage your weaknesses. Delegate those skills you are weak at to those who are better adept. Find someone who knows what they are doing, trust them, rely on them, and be thankful they're there.

I bet you always knew you were a superhero, even as a kid.

Crisis: Not Fulfilling Your Childhood Dreams

A man is not old until regrets take the place of dreams.
—John Barrymore

Not so long ago, Marc and I went to the Jersey Shore with some friends for the weekend. As we sat in the sand on Long Beach Island in New Jersey watching the blue waves roll in, Tim, our friend for over twenty years, asked me what I had wanted to be when I was a kid. I remarked that no one had asked me that question before, so I needed to think about it for a bit. Soon enough my mind returned to fourth grade, when I proudly announced to my friend Debbie that I was going to be a teacher, but in the summer I'd work as a cruise director, just like Julie McCoy from my favorite television show at the time, *The Love Boat*. I also thought I'd like to be a truck driver like BJ McKay from another favorite show, *BJ and the Bear*. Both Julie and BJ inspired me to travel, have adventures, and dream of what my future as a grown-up could become.

Tim smiled as I relayed the story. When I finished, he said, "Well, I guess you fulfilled that."

I looked at him quizzically. Had he even heard what I'd just said? I didn't do any of those things. Sure, I had been a substitute teacher at Eric and Jena's school over the years, and yes, I had taken a few vacation cruises. And my father-in-law was a truck driver, but me? Nope. I never fulfilled any of those childhood dreams. Tim was way off. The sun and that drink he'd had at lunch must have gone straight to his head! I told him I didn't understand where he was coming from.

"Sure, Margarete, maybe you never worked those specific jobs," he continued, "but you travel the world, you've had lots of adventures, and you teach something to every single person you meet."

Hmm, I thought, *maybe I did fulfill my childhood dreams.* I never thought of it that way.

Kids Say the Darnedest Things

When my children were young, I asked them n what they wanted to be when they grew up. Eric, who was in kindergarten at the time, told me he wanted to be a major league baseball player or the person who works the drive-through window at McDonald's. When I asked him why he picked those two jobs, he replied it was because the people looked so happy making other people happy. Wow. Out of the mouth of babes. His dream was to find a way to make himself happy by making other people happy. At twenty-eight, his career as a financial planner fits well with this. Every day he's helping people save for retirement, plan for college expenses, and become financially secure. I'd say he's well on his way accomplishing what his five-year-old self wanted.

Jena, on the other hand, wanted to be a country music singer, an artist, and a teacher. She loved to be center stage wherever she went, and she had the shining personality that drew people to her. Jena wasn't gifted the time to fulfill those childhood dreams, but I'm sure she's singing songs, drawing beautiful nature scenes, and teaching the world from her resting place above.

Here's My Take

Childhood dreams are a lifeline to your inner passion, to what makes you tick. Without knowing it, your childhood inhibitions allow your thoughts to dream limitless possibilities. The ten-year-old me wanted to travel, and have fun adventures meeting new people. I loved school and learning, and what's better than sharing those things with other people? At the time, those career plans made sense to my childhood brain. After that talk with Tim, it now makes sense to my middle-aged mind.

Kids and teenagers have big imaginations with even bigger dreams. They have a reason behind wanting to be a mechanic or the president of the United States. Maybe they like fixing things, or perhaps they want to make a difference in the world. Maybe they admire someone who works in that field and it sparked an inner drive.

In my opinion, the most significant characteristic of being a young child is that children see without filters. Children are good role models for adults rather than the other way around. They speak from their hearts, and they don't set limits on what they want or what they think they can become. Kids dream of being their favorite superhero just as easily as they dream of becoming the kind and jovial bus driver who takes them to school each morning. Why, as adults, do we lose sight of that? What did we do with all that wonder and curiosity? Why do we close away those childhood dreams just because we've become adults? You're never too old to become the person you were meant to be. Don't let that childhood voice inside you be quiet. Give it a voice. Give it action. Give your childhood dreams wings, and let them take flight. You can make them come true if you want to. It's true. Pinkie-promise.

> You are never too old to set another goal or to dream a
> new dream.
>
> —C. S. Lewis

What's Your Take?

What was your childhood dream? Did you want to be an astronaut? A doctor? A drive-through worker at your local fast-food restaurant? Do you remember the reasons behind those goals and dreams? Does your life now reflect those reasons in some way? Might you have manifested those dreams in a way that your adult self doesn't recognize? Sometimes our oldest and dearest friends can see things in us that we can't. The next time you're with one of those friends, ask them!

Take It or Leave It

Get out your handy-dandy notebook and write down all the things you wanted to do as a kid. Go ahead. It's your notebook. No one will see that you wanted to run away and join the circus or live in a little house on the prairie like Laura Ingalls Wilder. Write down all the dreams you thought would come true and all the adventures you wanted to conquer, and then write down next to each one why you wanted it. Was it because you liked making people laugh or being outside in the natural world? Would you like to take some of the items from your long-ago list and put them on your midlife bucket list? Only you can decide to give them a chance and try to fulfill those passions. What better time to start being a kid than right now? Just remember, play nice in the sandbox!

Who knows, maybe you could just be the next contestant on *Survivor.*

Outwit, Outplay, Outlast

Don't Just Survive. Thrive!

Crisis:
Believing You're Not a Survivor

I am a huge fan of the CBS reality show *Survivor*. In 2000, it caught my attention, along with fifty million other people, and I thoroughly enjoyed watching Richard Hatch go full-monty in the first season to eventually win one million dollars. Talk about reality going raw and getting real! Every year since then, *Survivor* has brought sixteen contestants into our lives who, for thirty-nine days, compete and collaborate while pushing their physical, emotional, and problem-solving skills to the limit. Throughout the season, they experience what I affectionately call "speed existence," an abbreviated and adapted-for-TV version of the most challenging of reality shows, life.

Which of the contestants have the stamina to overcome the struggles? Who gets blindsided by a frenemy and voted off the island? What tribe has spoken to decide your immediate fate? And who is left to weather the next set of grueling challenges?

After watching week after week, season after season, as the participants break down, cry, swear, and sustain injuries, I would think more of them would give up. Wouldn't you? Yet they all want to stay in the game until the very end. They didn't come this far to call it quits just because the going was getting tough. Each contestant is there to win, and each of them must answer the question "How hard are you willing to work for it?" The answer is always the same: "Until."

Until they are voted out, are medevacked out, or eventually win. Throughout the days on the island, the camera crew interviews each person, and you, the viewer, get to see the physical and emotional transformation taking place. You see the physically weak utilizing their strength in wit, calculation, and charm. You see the muscularly strong break down when a loved one is flown in for support. You see the introverted break free from their shells and become leaders of their tribe. You see the reserved stretch outside their comfort zones to share stories, feelings, and strategies. Relationships are built, and deceit breaks the tightest of bonds. In the end, it's the person who can transform himself or herself, adapt to new situations, and work well with others in trust and authenticity who gains the most ground.

The contestants weather torrential rains and bitterly cold nights on a diet of rice and coconuts. They need to quickly acclimate to eating less and sleeping on sand or bamboo branches. If they win a challenge, they're rewarded with a tarp to keep them dry and possibly a wool blanket. "All the comforts of home," the host, Jeff Probst, says. Comforts, huh? While *Survivor* might be a television show, it's an awful lot like life.

There was a time when I felt I had been dumped on an island and I was full of despair. There was no prize money, no naked Richard Hatch, and no drive to survive. The island was my life, and the despair came from a decade of mothering children with cystic fibrosis, the fatal disease that ultimately claimed the life of my daughter, Jena. On this island, no Jeff Probst was handing me comforts. The island was harsh and painful, and I didn't want to be there. Despite wallowing in my misery, I managed to see the small glimpses of beauty the island contained. That beauty was found in my husband, my family, my son, and all the love that surrounded me.

I saw love in the form of friends helping me through the grieving. I saw hope in the form of prayer and meditation. I saw promise through the tiny steps of working to improve my mental outlook and emotional state. With each small challenge I conquered, I saw the blue skies, the lush and colorful landscape, and the open hearts of those around me. I started to win my own challenges of learning to love again, hoping and believing I could make it through another day on the island of life. And as each day went on, the joys began to outweigh the pain. I started to shed my fears and understand how these trials and challenges taught me what I'm made of. The shift I've made since the day I arrived on this island to get me to where I am now has been drastic. Pain, heartache, and death brought me here. But as Jena told me before she moved up to heaven, "Pain is not a valid reason for stopping." And that has been my mantra, my secret strategy for winning every season in this very personal version of *Survivor*. Persist through the pain because pain is not a valid reason for stopping.

I've learned to lean into the uncomfortable, to seek out where my comfort zone ends, and to trust in the kindness of strangers because I choose to live in a world that's good and worthy of love. I've learned to outwit the negativity, outlast my own limiting beliefs about what I could become, and outplay those who taught me valuable lessons by breaking my trust in them. Emotional pain hurts intensely, but it's a valuable teacher. It tells you when it's time to move forward or move away. It's your wake-up call to make a change.

I've learned to live with a passion greater than I'd ever felt possible. I've learned to press on, pursue, grow, and welcome the feelings of love and compassion. I now reside in a place of joy because I've lived with the pain of feeling unworthy, weak, and in despair. Now, as a real-life survivor, I've learned that all along I was a lot stronger than I ever gave myself credit for.

Here's My Take

Despite having the same genetic profile as Jena, my son, Eric, doesn't just survive; he thrives. He has outwitted, outlasted, and outplayed so many naysayers because his strength comes from within. He cannot control that he has cystic fibrosis, so he focuses on what he does have: a thriving career, loads of friends, a beautiful, supportive wife, and the optimism for a happy and long future. To be a successful survivor, you need to do *one* thing, and that one thing is to *keep going*. It's simple advice, but it's far from easy to implement. You need to make sure the thoughts in your head are encouraging you to keep going. You need to find someone or something to hold yourself accountable to. You need to keep moving and give a little more effort with every passing day. Remember, you can't be defeated if you don't give up. Keep going. Keep your head high. Keep smiling. And keep taking the steps to make those dreams a reality.

I'm often asked why I am so happy, and I generally respond by asking a question in return: "Why wouldn't I be?" People are often mystified that after so many years of battling cystic fibrosis on behalf of my children, I'm still upbeat and positive. Sometimes I tell them that if I could be sad enough, cry enough, and be miserable enough to bring Jena back, I would. But no matter what I do, she's not coming back, and I believe the best gift I can give her is to honor her spirit and embrace the life she fought so hard for. I've been given the gift of life, and because I'm still breathing, I'm going to make the most of it. I guess I enjoy *Survivor* so much because it helps me to love life even more. When you can move past the pain, you'll be amazed at what you uncover.

A crisis will always be there and is not reserved for just the middle-aged. So, I ask you three questions: Why are you *not* happy? How will you become your own survivor? And how are you getting off your island?

I know my worth now, I own my strength. I became a survivor. And I'm pretty sure you are a survivor too. You're here right now because you *are* a survivor.

What's Your Take?

Have you ever felt like life has turned into an episode of *Survivor*? Have you felt deceived, blindsided, or abandoned? Are you stronger or weaker for it? Does experiencing painful emotions freeze you in your tracks or spark you to make a change? All of us have been given challenges, and too often we are left not knowing whom to trust, questioning how to make it through another day, feeling sad and alone, and being uncertain about the next step. What is it that makes you most afraid? Is it what others may think? Is it fear of failure? Are you afraid to push yourself into an unknown area? Are you questioning your choices?

Give yourself time to reflect. How did you come to this place? Maybe you signed up for this adventure, or perhaps being on the "island" isn't by choice. But the fact is, you're here now. What have you learned? Moving forward, what is your intention? Why do you want what you are seeking? Be clear about what you want to bring into your life. Then take a moment and take stock of who you are and what you've already accomplished. How can you outlast, outwit, and outplay the latest setback? Ask yourself if you're utilizing your skills, be they social, physical, or emotional, to reach your goal. What's your inner or outer strength that can take you one step closer? What's one action you can do to move closer to where you want to be?

Take It or Leave It

When you work on yourself and start taking actions to pursue your dreams, a funny thing happens: so many of the puzzle pieces begin to fall into place. I don't know the origins, but I've heard it said that when you pray, make sure you move your feet. Take time to be still and reflective and to pray, but don't forget to act and move your feet. And while you're at it, give thanks for all your blessings, including the heartaches.

Share your life with others. I guarantee you will help someone who hears your story. It will change their life. Share your story. Share the real and raw you. You are and always have been good enough.

Write down your goals and what you want. Then write down *why* you want it. Be detailed in your answer. Keep that paper close by; you'll want to reflect on it every time you have the desire to give up. Don't give up. Never give up on yourself. Be big. Dream big. Even the smallest of pebbles makes waves.

Toss a pebble into the stillness of life and see what ripples you can make!

Off into the Sunset

Looking for the Little Things that Make Life Big

Crisis:
Never Experiencing
Appreciation and Gratitude

Well, friends, our journey has taken us to the final chapter of *Embracing the Beauty in the Broken*. I rarely say goodbye because I don't believe our stories, friendships, or love ever ends; it just shifts in a new direction. Together, we've now reached a point where our relationship is shifting. As you've wandered and worked your way through my stories, not only have you learned more about me, but also you've likely learned a lot about yourself and what you're capable of doing, being, and becoming.

As a parting gift, I think this is the perfect time to share with you a powerful ritual that is near and dear to me. I call it the "Hallelujah Sunset," and it began on the anniversary of Jena's passing.

Here's how it came to be:

It was the morning of December 4, 2014, and I was in Savannah, Georgia, with Marc, ready for the tsunami of grief-stricken emotions that usually flood my heart on this date. That December 4th marked eight years since Jena had moved up to heaven, and it was and will continue to be the one day of the year when I allow myself to be and feel anything I need to be and feel—and that includes not being and feeling fine.

But this particular December 4th was different.

Over breakfast, I told Marc, "I know Jena's spirit is alive in my heart, and I really feel we need to see the sunset over the ocean and toast our Jena, along with the beauty that is life, and the fact that love never ends."

Within ten minutes we were in the car in search of the perfect ocean sunset.

Six hours later we arrived at the Gulf of Mexico and checked into a hotel at 4:42 p.m., just in time to witness the start of a spectacular sunset from the room's balcony.

From the moment I walked into the room, I could feel Jena all around me. The emotion brought me to my knees. I was sobbing because even though I could feel her presence, I knew I would never hug, kiss, or see my daughter again in this lifetime. Slowly, I lifted myself from the floor and made my way to the balcony, where Marc was, and together we watched the most glorious sunset. Through our tears and smiles, we toasted the beauty of life and gave thanks that Jena's spirit would always remain alive and well in our hearts and souls.

That night was the first December fourth where I felt a sense of peace come over me. As I watched the sun sink below the horizon in all its vibrant colors, I felt as if Jena had personally led us here, that she wanted us to have a special gift that would make this day, and our future days, a bit less painful.

Peace is seeing a sunset and remembering whom to thank.

The experience on that day was so profound that I was drawn to return to the Gulf Coast for the next four years, escaping the cold New York winters for as long as possible. Being surrounded by the steady flow of ocean waves carried me to a place deep within my soul where I found serenity, tranquility, and peace. During those days and weeks, I wrote my second book, *See You a Sunset*, a fictional story inspired by Jena and the beauty of coastal Florida. The work of writing helped me to reconnect with a quiet joy inspired by a new sense of purpose.

Every night about ten minutes before sunset, I'd pour myself a glass of wine, cue up the song "Hallelujah" on my iTunes, and gaze out toward the horizon. I'd take a moment to reflect on all the blessings of the day, set an intention for the next day, and give thanks for everything in my life: the good, the bad, and the life lessons I was struggling with. Then, as the sun melted into the Gulf of Mexico, shining its amber glow across the deep blue sky, I'd offer a prayer up to the heavens, blow a kiss to my daughter, and ask that she watch over us all, sinners and saints, and help us to find peace. During my stay in Florida, I made time for this ritual every night, and soon, even if it was cloudy and there was no sunset visible to my eyes, my thoughts stayed the same. And that's how the "Hallelujah Sunset" became a part of my daily spiritual practice. No matter where I am when the day ends, I want to be thankful for having lived it, and each morning I want to feel gratitude for another day with the people who love me.

You might not have a balcony on the ocean or live in a place where you can easily see the sunset, but I suggest you give a version of this practice a try. Whether it's after dinner or before bed, give yourself a few minutes to offer thanks for all that transpired over the past day, and then set an intention for the next one. As you finish the day, you'll feel supported in knowing that you can handle anything the sunrise will bring.

How do I know you'll survive and thrive amid whatever challenges and opportunities each day brings? Because you have successfully survived all that life has brought you thus far; you're alive, you're breathing, and you're here. You can face the day ahead and offer thanks for the lessons of the past. You can survive and thrive. You can live the life you want with help from your beautiful parts, your broken parts, and the gift of time that has been granted to you.

When you stop and think about it, isn't that what life is all about? When you connect to the source inside of you with gratitude and appreciation, you return to the world a little stronger, a little more centered, a little more capable of helping not only yourself but also others on their journey through life.

I hope that by writing *Embracing the Beauty in the Broken*, I have helped you find strength and confidence to move forward through these midlife years in a bold and passion-filled way. I hope by giving you some of me, the raw, real, and rarely quiet me, I have led you to open up your heart to the raw, real, and rarely quiet you. You're now a part of a community of midlife women who want to make this world and our time in it better for everyone. If you are so moved, reach out to me, let me know what you think, and say hello. I'd love to hear from you.

Remember the quotation I mentioned in the introduction to *Embracing the Beauty in the Broken*?

> Someone once told me the definition of Hell: The last day you have on earth, the person you became will meet the person you could have become.
>
> —Anonymous

Well, how do you feel about it now? I know I've changed the way I view this quotation. When the sun sets for the final time in your life, I hope you are met by the person the Creator intended you to be. I hope that you are then able to see how far you've come, how strong you are, and how you seized the day each day the gift of life was with you. I hope that the day is a blessing and that the person you meet is the person you would have become had you not found the strength, took the action, and knew that you could become the best possible you this life could offer.

Breathe.

Be thankful.

And be blessed.

See you at sunset!

Take It or Leave It

I've saved my all-time favorite exercise for this chapter! It's called the Name Game, and it's a fun way to remember your worth and what you are made of.

Here's what you do:

Write out your name one letter at a time, going down the page, and for each letter, write a word that describes who you are and who you want to be. Each letter can describe the unique qualities that make you authentic, strong, and filled with passion.

Here's the exercise using my name:

M – Mother
A – Authentic
R – Romantic
G – Go-getter
A – Athletic
R – Resilient
E – Energetic
T – Trusting
E – Empathic

Remember, there is no one else who's quite like you! Your unique qualities have the power to shine a light into someone else's darkness. Be brave, be the light, and embrace the beauty in the broken.

CPSIA information can be obtained
at www.ICGtesting.com
Printed in the USA
FFHW022145221019
55711674-61563FF